Jomon of Japan

Jomon of Japan
The World's Oldest Pottery

Douglas Moore Kenrick

Kegan Paul International
London and New York

First published in 1995 by
Kegan Paul International Limited
UK: P.O. Box 256, London WC1B 3SW, England
USA: 562 West 113th Street, New York, NY 10025, USA

Distributed by
John Wiley & Sons Limited
Southern Cross Trading Estate
1 Oldlands Way, Bognor Regis
West Sussex, PO22 9SA, England

Columbia University Press
562 West 113th Street
New York, NY 10025, USA

© Douglas Moore Kenrick 1995

Set in 11 on 13pt Bembo
by Selwood Systems, Midsomer Norton

Printed in Great Britain by Butler & Tanner Ltd, Frome and London

ISBN 0 7103 0475 7

British Library Cataloguing in Publication Data

Kenrick, Douglas Moore
Jomon of Japan: The World's Oldest Pottery
I. Title
738.0952

ISBN 0-7103-0475-7

US Library of Congress Cataloging in Publication Data

Kenrick, Douglas M.
Jomon of Japan : the world's oldest pottery / Douglas Moore
Kenrick.
150 pp. 25 cm.
Includes bibliographical references (p. 72) and index.
ISBN 0-7103-0475-7 : £45 ($76.50)
1. Pottery, Jōmon——Catalogs.   2. Pottery, Japanese——To 794—
—Catalogs.   3. Pottery——Japan——Catalogs.   I. Title.
NK4167.22.K46   1994
738.3'0952'09012——dc20

94–2521
CIP

Contents

Foreword

The carbon-14 dates for pottery from the Natsushima shell-mound hit the world of Japanese archaeology in 1960 like a bolt out of the blue. Their antiquity was met with almost total disbelief, in Japan because of the traditional and centuries-old view that cultural innovations were Chinese-inspired and no older dates for Chinese ceramics were known, and elsewhere because the whole idea of a small, peripheral area contributing a major invention to the world's ancient cultures was virtually unthinkable.

The 'carbon-14 shock', as it came to be known, were dates for the pottery of the Natsushima shell-mound at Yokosuka in Kanagawa prefecture. One charcoal sample was placed at 9240 ± 500 Before Present (BP) (or 7290 ± 500 BC), and a shell sample at 9450 ± 400 BP (or 7500 ± 400 BC). The shell-mound had three separate ceramic-bearing layers, but in all cases the pottery types belonged exclusively to Earliest (alternatively Initial) Jomon. In retrospect, one can only see it as fortuitous that these dates were determined in the University of Michigan laboratory, a laboratory already well established in supplying acceptable dates to American archaeologists and thus with a credibility that might otherwise have been doubted. Japanese laboratories did not get into the business of testing for several years; had it been a Japanese laboratory that first published such results it would have been widely distrusted as politically slanted, leaving a cloud of suspicion that may have never vanished.

It was pointed out early that shell would then produce less reliable results, but neither of the two dates could be explained away, and I found myself at international meetings defending the dates against charges of contamination, faulty collecting methods, distortion from volcanic action, and other criticisms. My defences were partly to convince myself that we were on the right track and more lay down the road, and partly because it was all so new, other Asianists had legitimate questions about what stance archaeologists were willing to take. I even recall one sinologist – whose views of Japan are to a great extent justified – referring to the process of accepting these old dates for Japanese ceramics as a 'traumatic experience'.

Little time elapsed before a group in Japan rejected the early dates and established what they called the 'short chronology', but by the later 1960s Natsushima began to pale in the light of older dates for the new line of pottery types being unearthed in rock-shelter and cave sites. To accommodate these new types, Japanese archaeologists added an older stage to the framework of five stages of the Jomon period, its originator ironically the leader of the 'short chronology' school. It is a stage I have called Subearliest in my writings (alternatively Incipient), and it put Natsushima on the irrelevant shelf. Not only were these dates fitting stratigraphically with the earlier types, they conformed to both the accepted stylistic evolution of these newly discovered types and their geographical spread.

This point had been reached in a new era of chronology construction in prehistoric archaeology. Refinements of existing methods and new dating techniques were being tried for their usefulness – obsidian hydration, fission-track dating, thermoluminescence (TL) and thermoremanent magnetism (TRM) – and half-life adjustments, calibration and other modifications were being made in the carbon-14 laboratories. Cross-checking, formerly often done against historical data such as ancient Egyptian and Near Eastern history, was now in terms of other scientific techniques. Fresh arguments were generated, but the value in these older dates for Jomon pottery lay in the fact that widely scattered and quite independent laboratories were providing dates that fell right into place within the sequence. Using charcoal samples gathered from layers associated with Subearliest Jomon pottery in the Kamikuroiwa rock-shelter, Iwashita cave and Fukui cave, all in southwest Japan, the Smithsonian Institution, Isotopes and Gakushuin (Tokyo) laboratories placed a range of four dates between 10,085 ± 320 and 12,700 ± 500 BP. It is surely no coincidence that the invention of pottery occurred at this time of great environmental change – the retreat of the last glaciers – when considerable human adjustment and ingenuity were required for survival.

When I did my first Jomon pottery book in the 1950s (*The Jomon Pottery of Japan*, Artibus Asiae, Ascona, 1959), nothing but vague ideas on relative dating existed. The best one could do was deal with typological sequences and the sites that had been well excavated stratigraphically and so suggest a few dates, trying to fit them with other factors of east Asian prehistory. The problems had no solutions. But the story had changed dramatically by the later 1960s when the opportunity came to write *Prehistoric Japanese Arts: Jomon Pottery* (Kodansha International, Tokyo, 1968). By that time scores of carbon-14 dates were available for the entire Jomon period and one felt confident of working within a solid chronometric framework. Nevertheless, it did not seem to be the occasion to make the great age of the pottery an issue in itself. Interestingly, the Japanese had never appeared to be able quite to overcome a certain unease about bearing the burden of the world's oldest pottery, probably because they expected to wake up some day to find it was all only a pleasant dream.

Eras come and go, the idea is more settling to this generation of archaeologists, new dates fill out world chronologies, and yet older ones do not appear. The occasion to see the Japanese contribution in its world perspective is long overdue, and I am pleased that this task has been ably undertaken by Dr Douglas Kenrick, a long-time resident of Tokyo and for many years involved in various ways with ancient Japanese ceramics. Jomon pottery, even ignoring its remarkable antiquity, is in any case an amazing cultural phenomenon, and it is gratifying that it is now being given its rightful place in the ancient cultures of the world.

J. Edward Kidder, Jr
Professor Emeritus,
International Christian University, Tokyo

Preface

The Jomon people of Japan, a hunter and gatherer culture, produced pottery[1] cooking vessels at least two thousand years before pottery was made anywhere else in the world.

Pottery has played a significant role in cultural development worldwide and, over the ages, has produced treasure troves of beautiful objects. About ninety per cent of all Jomon vessels display surface decorations, many of remarkable beauty.

For prehistoric peoples, as they moved along the road towards cuvilization, the creation of earthenware cooking vessels could have been as momentous as the invention of the wheel. The introduction of cooking pots was, of course, only one of many developments, but its contribution should not be underrated. (Today we take fireproof cooking vessels for granted. Just think what our meals would be like without them.)

To nomadic peoples who travelled long distances in search of food, breakages of fragile pots could have negated their advantages until people began a more settled life. The Jomon hunter–gatherers had not needed to roam far to obtain sustenance. Later, when other prehistoric peoples tied themselves to cultivating plants and domesticating animals, fireproof pottery cooking vessels became a central part of all household life.

Jomon vessels stand on their own merits of form and textured decoration, as these potters' works are not hidden by colourful glazed surfaces. They remain in 'their original naked grandeur', as Wildenhain once put it. Inspection of unglazed earthenware pots brings us back to the spirit of the potters, the working of clay, and its firing. It makes us very aware of the different results that come from individuals working in isolation, of the temperatures they achieved within their bonfires, and their control, if any, over the supply of oxygen to the fire. Jomon vessels may have little immediate attraction to those who judge pots by the beauty of their glaze, but unglazed vessels can reveal qualities which generate their own appeal.

From about 10,000 BC until almost the beginning of the Christian era, the Jomon, with little essential change, made pottery in open fires. Open-fired pots are rarely exactly the same colour all over. From different clays, surfaces range from off-white and grey through buff, reddish-brown to black. The pots acquire their colour from the minerals in the clay, notably iron, the heat of the flames, and their contact with embers and ash. They retain it as they cool to what is often a mottled buff with patches burned black.

It requires imagination to begin to comprehend the length and vitality of the Jomon pottery age. Age leaves its mark on vessels buried for so long, but a feeling of awe at the age of a vessel should not blind us to its beauty, or lack of beauty. However, consciousness of the pots' sheer antiquity may arouse interest not only in the pots themselves but also in the techniques of the artisans, and the cultures of the users.

The Jomon potters lived in intimate closeness to the vessels they made and used but they were not artists creating for display only. On present evidence, it appears that most Jomon pots played their role in the basic subsistence of the people. However, some vessels are found in contexts that leave little room for interpretation unrelated to ritual usage. Gill (1982) has emphasized that, to primitive human beings, art was not an isolated aspect of their culture but was embedded in useful and ceremonial objects. Ancient pottery is often referred to as being utilitarian and crude. Jomon vessels were functional, even when made for rituals.

Yanagi wrote:

> By use, then, I intend the indivisibility of mind and matter. . . . The special quality of beauty in crafts is that it is a beauty of intimacy. . . . Such beauty established a world of grace and feeling. Things made that do not stand up to use or that ignore utility can barely be expected to contain this kind of beauty.

Jomon pottery had to give daily service. It was on view and subject to constant appraisal. All members of the household could and, and no doubt, did criticize the utility, convenience of handling, porosity, durability and appearance of every pot. All the evidence suggests that the makers were part-time potters within a family circle of users. Decoration, shapes and sizes combine as one the users' tastes and the potters' skill. Some Jomon household wares were crude, but many were remarkably refined.

In addition to skill, Jomon pots show the remarkable invention and sensitivity of their makers. (In Japan it was not until the adoption of agriculture, about 300 BC, that plain surfaces became common.) Why did the Jomon potters embellish their pots? If most pots were purely utilitarian, why adorn their surfaces? Irregular surfaces could have made handling more easy, but the potters must also have desired to make their wares attractive to the eye. Just as the undecorated pots of the later agricultural period may indicate pressure on time, so the elaborate decoration of the Jomon pots is surely evidence of considerable leisure.

Modern communications have brought Japan very close to Europe and America but, even today, the Far East of antiquity remains remote from the thinking of much of the world. Although museums in many countries have a few specimens, the West knows little of the early unglazed earthenware of Japan. When Westerners consider the prehistoric pottery of Japan and her neighbours, China and Korea, this vast area should not be thought of as a single entity.

Some of the lack of awareness in the West is due to very little having been recently written in English about the earliest pottery of the isolated Jomon culture of the Japanese islands. In 1968 J. Edward Kidder published his monumental *Prehistoric Japanese Arts: Jomon Pottery*, and has given pre-eminence to Jomon pottery in a number of his other publications. C. Melvin Aikens and Takayasu Higuchi have included references to pottery in *The Prehistory of Japan* (1982). A wide-ranging account, *Windows on the Japanese Past*, edited by Richard J. Pearson (1986), also includes essays on Jomon pottery. More recently Kiyotari Tsuboi and Shimpei Kato have written briefly about Jomon pottery in *Recent Archaeological Discoveries in Japan* (1987). However, these books are very rarely found in Western libraries. They are specialized and often expensive.

In contrast to the small handful of reference works about Jomon pottery in English, archaeologists and ceramicists have produced a very lengthy bibliography in Japanese. Tatsuo Kobayashi's four-part series, *Jomon doki taikan* (A survey of Jomon Pottery) (1988, 1989) is most relevant. It has an excellent text, unfortunately in Japanese only, but contains about 200 colour and about 6,000 black and white illustrations.

Many hundreds of thousands of Jomon vessels have been excavated but very few can be found in Western museums and collections. However, there are some, and anyone who comes to Japan can visit the ubiquitous museums and the many universities and archaeological research centres. On view are hundreds of Jomon pots of all phases, with the advantage that the local museums bring them close to the setting where the pots were found. In Japan all archaeological materials are considered to be national property, but they may be held by individuals as long as they take proper care of them. Jomon wares are available to be appreciated.

This book aims to give a condensed, overall view of Jomon pottery itself, and its relation to the ancient pottery of other countries. The oldest Jomon pots appear to have the distinction of being much older than those yet found anywhere else in the world. This book does not go into details of the sources of possible error in dates at present widely accepted. Neither does it give a verdict on which of the many Jomon sites has yielded the oldest pottery of all. Such research deserves a separate book. That the most ancient Jomon pottery was invented about 10,000 BC has been acknowledged by leading Western archaeologists for more than a decade. Since Grahame Clark wrote *World Prehistory* (1977:324) many more ancient sites have been excavated in Japan and the age of their pottery determined by scientific tests.

It is appropriate to compare Jomon with the oldest pottery of other regions. This is done briefly in the first part of this book. The sections that follow give thumbnail sketches of the development of pottery-making in Japan over an immense timespan of about ten thousand years.

(In this book, following Western convention, Japanese given names are placed first and family names second. The Kanji characters of a number of Japanese terms are included in the end notes, n.8.)

Acknowledgements

The book owes much to so many. I have been fortunate to have had frequent and wholehearted help from many experienced archaeologists and art historians.

The criticisms, ideas and suggestions of additional sources of information by Professor Charles T. Keally, Sophia University, Tokyo, have played a large part in shaping this book. My debt is expressed here in a very sincere acknowledgement. Professor J. Edward Kidder, International Christian University, Tokyo, has also been ungrudging with his thoughtful comments and valuable suggestions. Professor Kidder's *Prehistoric Japanese Arts: Jomon Pottery*, published in 1968, is the one classic work that has been published in English on the subject. Professor Tatsuo Kobayashi, Kokugakuin University, Tokyo, author and editor of many articles and books on Jomon pottery, has been a constant and invaluable adviser and friendly critic. He has provided many splendid illustrations and the Kanji characters for Japanese words; Edward Field, as a referee appointed by the British Institute of Archaeology, has done yeoman service. He has given his time unstintingly in suggesting many changes in the structure and details of this work. His guidance has been tremendously helpful. Messrs Keally, Kidder, Kobayashi and Field could all claim joint authorship, their help has been so great. However, the text gives my interpretations and its shortcomings are my responsibility. I express here my gratitude and good fortune in having the guidance of such acknowledged experts in the field of Jomon pottery and all that is associated with it.

Dr Ian C. Glover, James Mellaart and P. J. Parr of the British Institute of Archaeology, University College, University of London, have all been extremely generous, going far beyond the calls of duty, imparting their deep knowledge of the archaeology and ceramics of Western Asia; Dr Peter H. Plesch of the University of Keele has made very valuable comments on the manuscript.

Dr An Zhimin, of the Institute of Archaeology, Chinese Academy of Social Sciences, has given much helpful advice on prehistoric Chinese pottery; Dr Kim Won-yong, former Dean of the Graduate School, Seoul National University, has kindly endorsed my choice of data and interpretation of his studies as recorded in his *Art and Archaeology of Ancient Korea* (1986); Dr Im Hyo-jai, Curator of the Seoul National University Museum, has supplied photographs of vessels from his excavations at Osan-ri; Professor Lee Hee-joon has made most helpful suggestions.

Kenji Fukuda, Tokyo Metropolitan Archaeological Department, has given good advice and selected and drawn for this book a range of pottery jars illustrative of the whole Jomon period; Chosuke Serizawa, Professor Emeritus, Yohoku University, and Professor Kohei Kitano, Kobe Mercantile Marine University, have been ungrudging, friendly and helpful in giving their unstinted, kindly answers to my many questions and in making useful suggestions on matters I had not raised. The associates of the late Dr C. F. Gorman at the University of Pennsylvania (which holds the Spirit Cave sherds), and Dr David J. Welch of the University of Hawaii, have also been extremely helpful; Professor Richard J. Pearson, University of British Columbia, has given very useful advice; Professor Kidder, Makoto Sahara and Kodansha International have most generously permitted use of illustrations from Kidder's *Prehistoric Japanese Arts: Jomon Pottery* and Sahara's *Jomon doki taisei* (Complete guide to Jomon pottery); thanks also to the expert photographer Yoji Ando.

So many more experts have been consulted that it is difficult to name them all, but without their guidance and assistance this book would have been an even less adequate condensation of the present body of changing knowledge of the early pottery of Japan.

My secretary Yoko Nishikata deserves more thanks than I can convey. I have relied on her unfailing help and her critical suggestions and guidance as she assisted in typing and retyping this book as it has been written and rewritten. Tamiko Hamada and Toyoko Noiro, also my secretaries, have also given very great assistance in typing many further revisions.

The World's Oldest Pottery

Scientific Dating

Until quite recently archaeologists estimated the ages of pots and other artefacts by typology and from the successive strata in which the vessels were found. They showed remarkable skill in establishing and comparing sequences. However, it is today generally agreed that they were often adrift in their assumptions of prehistoric chronology and comparative dating. Since the 1950s a number of scientific methods of testing the absolute age of artefacts are being employed: radiocarbon (C14), thermoluminescence (TL), obsidian fission-track (FT), obsidian hydration (OB). Geological, palaeoclimatological and other means are also used. Another general guide used in Japan is tephrochronology, which is the dating of volcanic ash layers from the different eruptions of the distant past. A firm chronology in calendar years BC may be provided by these various means.

The old method of guessing dates has been superseded but scientific dating is not yet infallible. Thermoluminescence figures may require adjustment as sites must be tested thoroughly. This may take a team six months of intensive testing and this has not been carried out on all sites. Obsidian hydration dates are treated with caution as they can be very variable.

It is worth stressing that, at present, radiocarbon dates cannot be obtained directly from pottery unless charred remains of food are contained within. (Such circumstances are extremely rare). C14 testing is therefore usually applied to any organic material found with the pottery, e.g. shell, bone, antler or charcoal. In this way C14 pottery dates are deduced from their association with organic finds from within the same stratum or context.

Radiocarbon dates may be calibrated by comparison with the dating of tree-rings of known age. However, the longest known sequence of tree-rings extends back only for the past 8,000 years. Beyond that age there are too few samples of wood to construct a valid sequence for earlier dates. It follows that as calibration cannot be used for the first 4,000 years of the Jomon period, it has not been used at all in this book for C14 dates for Japan.

Present dating of prehistoric artefacts, and the soils and organic materials they are found with, have still to be qualified by tolerances and these can be typically plus or minus 500 years. For the most ancient sites, the results of scientific tests at our present level of knowledge may disappoint the innocent enquirer who expects precision in the dating of 12,000-year-old objects. However, the scientific community now accepts that sherds from Fukui, Sempukuji, Kamikuroiwa, Kamino and some other sites in Japan really are from pottery made 'about 10,000 BC'.

Uncertainties can arise in various ways, such as an inadequate number of tests or insufficiently known regional environmental characteristics. There are always the possibilities of intrusions from one stratum to another. These can be from geological disturbance (volcanic and others), or from materials such as calcium carbonate in solutions that could have moved between strata. Climate, particularly temperature, also affects radiocarbon dates. Shell is known to be less reliable than charcoal because it can sometimes absorb solutions of older calcium carbonate from nearby limestone.

Dates from related artefacts in the same stratum rarely correspond exactly when tested by *different* scientific methods. Also, the *same* testing method may reveal, within a batch, a sample that dates very differently from the others. It is now common practice to suspect such an aberrant sample as an intrusion and to disregard it. Because of intrusions a single sample should not be relied on. In short, the dates given to ceramic sherds and vessels should be viewed with a measure of scepticism unless a series of tests produced a batch of results that are reasonably similar.

A very few specialists in Japanese archaeology still do not accept the new scientific findings. They quote the wide variations in a few results from radiocarbon tests on associated samples as evidence of a worldwide unreliability of *all* dates arrived at by scientific measurements. They still limit themselves to constructing sequences of pottery form and decoration which are not truly anchored in time.

Supporters of scientific dating take the view that a range of findings is fully acceptable when a number of tests have been run on multiple samples and ranges or median figures deduced. All prehistoric calendar year dates must be treated with reserve, but even the present state of our knowledge makes it irresponsible for us to ignore scientific datings. Approximate as these may be, they at least add relevance to the pottery sequences in Japan.

Now that scientific methods of absolute dating have been shown to be generally reliable, it has become feasible to make chronological comparisons between the regions of the Old World, and to estimate which were the earliest to produce pottery. A difference of as much as two thousand years in the earliest recorded dates between regions is now considered by the scientific community confidently to justify an assumption that the pottery of one region predates that of another.

The Invention of Pottery

The creation of pottery did not come for many, many millennia after the harnessing of fire despite the ever-present opportunity to make fuller and better use of food resources by the invention of fireproof cooking vessels. Sun-dried vessels for storage might have come first but, except in Western Asia, have left no trace yet found by archaeologists. The inspiration to make pottery by firing clay could have come from observation of the properties of clay hardened around fireplaces, or the shape taken by sun-dried clay plastered around woven baskets, but so far there is no evidence of pottery in Palaeolithic assemblages. The invention could have been triggered by a conscious need, or by a stray chance when an ingenious and inventive individual created a fired clay pot.

Improved cooking methods saved labour. Boiled foods are more digestible than raw or roasted foods. Cooking in water introduced a widening range of new flavours from fish, meat, nuts, fruits, leaves and tubers. Boiling is an advantage when preparing shellfish. Bamboo shoots are made edible, and certain yams are toxic if not boiled. Boiled foods reduce the weaning time of infants and release their mothers from protracted breast-feeding. Old people who have lost teeth are given new leases of life. In addition to improving diet, sterilization by boiling water reduces contamination, food poisoning and the spread of disease.

The emergence of the first pottery has been assumed by many archaeologists in the past to have occurred about the time that a culture changed from reliance on hunting and gathering to the cultivation of crops, particularly grain crops, and the adoption of the more settled life demanded by agriculture. The change seems to have taken place in north China in this way, but in Japan the hunting, gathering and fishing culture of the Jomon period continued in an unbroken line without systematic agriculture for about ten millennia after the indigenous creation of cooking pots. Perhaps an abundance of natural foods for a relatively small population in Japan made the laborious cultivation of grain unnecessary and unattractive even though the people become sedentary. At the other extreme, in Western Asia there might have been a gap of up to two thousand years after grain cultivation and before the invention of pottery.

Pottery-making could have started independently in many parts of the world, or it could have begun in a single area from which the technique spread far and wide. Taking the world as a whole, scientific methods of estimating dates support the first possibility. There appears to be a number of widely separated centres of varying ages where the pottery is considerably earlier than in the surrounding or intervening areas. The obvious interpretation is that once ceramic technology was discovered in one location, such knowledge radiated, or diffused, throughout that region, no matter how slowly.

To trace interactions between cultures, whether on a world scale or within regions, we need time-frames. The oldest pottery dates currently accepted may be extended by new finds, and all scientifically estimated dates (especially those earlier than 5,000 BC) have still to be treated with discretion.

Present evidence indicates that cooking pots were invented independently in at least three parts of the world, Japan, Western Asia, South America and probably in China, and perhaps in the Soviet Union, and in Korea.

In these regions the oldest pottery datings are at present estimated to be about:

Japan 10,000 BC, Western Asia 7,600 BC, China 8,000 or 6,500 BC, Siberia possibly about 10,000 BC, and Korea 6,000 to 4,500 BC, South America 4,000 BC. Origins in these regions, omitting South America, will be discussed briefly before commenting at greater length on the Jomon pottery of Japan.

Regions

Japan   In contrast to the paucity of writings in English about Japan, up to 1,500 excavation reports in Japanese have been published each year during the last few years. In addition there are articles in dozens of national, regional and local archaeological periodicals. Newspaper articles are now collected and published in a monthly magazine of more than 150 pages of small print each issue. In the *Kokogaku janaru* (Archaeological journal) February 1987, Kenji Fukuda summarized reports for 1986 from over 100 major excavations in that year. All this reflects a mind-boggling amount of archaeological activity, probably more intensive than in any other country in the world.

In Japan there are nearly 4,000 archaeologists of whom almost 2,000 are employed full time in archaeological work. No one knows the number of field-workers, many of whom are full-time contract labour. Estimates range from 20,000 to 50,000. Japan allocates an astronomical total annual budget for archaeology and it is rising rapidly. There are estimated to be over 300,000 archaeological sites registered, over 4,000 in Tokyo alone. About 10,000 large and small excavations are said to be in progress every year.

Over the whole field of their activities we might expect Japanese scholars to have reached a consensus in defining the dating and classification of all prehistoric and protohistoric Japanese pottery. However, the volume of the work being done makes it an almost impossible task for specialists to keep fully abreast of, and to digest, the mass of information being produced by unco-ordinated organizations, teams and individuals. The number of researchers is so large that they have grouped implacably around competing senior archaeologists whose opinions differ, but are strongly voiced. These 'schools' have built barriers against reaching an overall consensus.

The Japanese work in cliques which observe rigid conformity within them-selves, but each clique competes against all other cliques. Conflicting conclusions are held by different groups on many relevant matters, particularly relating to prehistoric and protohistoric dates, and there has been little endeavour to reconcile them. What attempts have been made seem often to have ended where they started, each side still clinging to its original ideas. A reluctance to debate is an obstacle. To question assumptions is thought to cast doubt, not on the assumptions, but on the integrity and sincerity of the persons who voice them. Information from new discoveries, the reinterpretation of the evidence from old excavations, and even the recent analyses of the mineral contents of clays, are still being assimilated. The findings of archaeologists and ceramicists have not yet been, and show no signs of being, welded into a generally accepted body of knowledge concerning prehistoric pottery.

To many Japanese, prehistory is still hidden in clouds of myth and uncertainty, but local archaeologists have been piecing it together in considerable detail in recent years. The origins of the first inhabitants of Japan are not agreed upon, but it is now accepted as common knowledge that human beings were in the islands by about 50,000 BC at the latest. Much earlier dates are still debated. There are those who argue convincingly that, with the exception of Hokkaido, none of the main islands of the archipelago have been connected to the continent for at least 100,000 years. Before 10,000 BC or earlier, when the earliest recorded pottery was made, the sea had engulfed any land-bridges that might have remained and had created a natural barrier between Japan and the mainland.

Jomon potters were established in Kyushu, with earliest dates which tend to reach about 10,500 BC, and central and northern Honshu, where several sites appear to have dates of about 11,000 BC. Pottery reached Hokkaido further north but not until about 6,000 BC. The most ancient pottery is rare, being limited to scattered small sherds. The amount of pottery found in sites increases slowly until about 7,500 BC when it becomes an outstanding part of every site. The geographic distribution is evidence that from surprisingly ancient times the forebears of the Japanese achieved a widespread skill in producing pottery, and it also demonstrates their dependence upon pottery in the preparation of food.

In the light of present knowledge, the world's oldest pottery was invented by hunter-gathers who had not learned to cultivate grains, to domesticate animals, or even to settle in large villages. Many of the earliest pottery sherds in Japan have been found in small caves and rock-shelters. During the whole long Jomon period, most groupings at any one time were no larger than five to ten dwellings and were unlikely to have had more than about twenty-five to fifty people. Of equal pottery-making significance, nowhere else in the world was low-fired earthenware produced in open fires for so long before the invention or introduction of enclosed kilns and the making of higher-fired wares.

The Jomon period is now divided into six phases. These will be discussed in more detail after the following notes about discoveries of ancient pottery in other parts of the world.

Western Asia

Although there has been a great deal of exploration and excavation of prehistoric sites in Western Asia, only a fraction of the findings has been published. In some of the reports that are published, the innovation of pottery-making and descriptions of the pottery found tend to be submerged in the evidence of other cultural developments.

In many parts of Western Asia the establishment of large villages, the growing of wheat and barley, and the domestication of cattle, sheep or goats do not appear to have been accompanied by the making of pottery cooking vessels. The time-lag may have been as much as two thousand years. During these years the dry heat of Western Asia led to the sun-drying of clay bricks as an early building material, and apparently this climate also prompted some use of dried clay objects in households. Long before fired pottery cooking vessels were introduced anywhere in the region, some villages had substantial architecture and had grown almost to the size of towns. Why pottery cooking vessels were not in household use earlier in this part of the world is a mystery which has yet to be clarified.

Dried clay objects, probably used as storage vessels, would have lost their form if exposed to moisture but, in some parts of Western Asia, the extremely dry atmosphere has allowed a few sherds to survive over the millennia. The preservation of some originally unfired sherds may also be attributed to their being hardened unintentionally when the houses they were in burned down.

The sun-dried vessels indicated by the few surviving sherds are not considered by archaeologists as having been intended as pottery that had somehow been left unfired (in the greenware stage, to use the potter's term). Instead, these vessels are seen as the finished artefacts of a culture that had yet to discover the firing process that converts clay to pottery. Although vulnerable to dampness, sun-dried vessels were probably useful for storing grain, but would have been too fragile for moving around.

In considering pottery dating, it should be borne in mind that quoted radio-carbon dates may or may not be calibrated. The dates in this section are from an unpublished paper by James Mellaart, 1988. He has added 1,000 years to raw radiocarbon dates. His dates appear to be the oldest yet given the Western Asian pottery. Many other archaeologists are not convinced that calibration of dates older than 6,000 BC can be accepted with assurance.

Sherds of unfired clay vessels have been recovered from at least four sites located from Syria and South Jordan to Iran. Mureybet in northern Syria has yielded sherds of unfired clay vessels, the oldest so far reported. After calibration, they are dated about 8,600 BC. Çayonu in eastern Turkey, north of Mureybet, and Ganjdareh, far to the west in Iran, are both dated nearer to about 8,000 BC. A fourth site, at Beidha, in Jordan near the border with Israel, and well south of Mureybet, had sherds of unfired clay vessels a little more recent in date, about 7,600 BC (Mellaart, unpublished, 1988). None can be regarded as pottery. They are mentioned here as early examples of the forming of clay into useful shapes.

There is little doubt that earlier pottery will be found but, at the time of this writing, the earliest pottery-making in Western Asia may be typified by vessels excavated at Tell Aswad in northern Syria. The earliest Tell Aswad pots are coarse and poorly made but some have polished surfaces and later vessels from this site have painted decoration.

Of about the same date as Tell Aswad, about 7,500/7,250 BC (calibrated) there are at least six other pottery sites: Çatal Hüyük (southern Anatolia, Turkey); Amuq (north-western Syria); Bouqras (eastern Syria); Umm Dabaghiyah (Iraq); Tell Arpachiyah (Iraq); and Tepe Guran (Iran) (Mellaart, unpublished, 1988). These sites stretch over the whole width of Western Asia and the earliest pottery at each appears to have been produced about the same time.

Westwards, pottery is believed to have moved from Western Asia into Europe. The earliest pottery in Greece is said to date from about 5,000 BC. Eastwards, to the Indian sub-continent, possible transmission was probably about the same time. Of Indian, Allchin (1982) has written:

> The earliest evidence of pottery vessels has been found at Mehrgarh, on the banks of the Bolan river near Sibi, not far from the point where the river emerges through a gorge from the valleys of Baluchistan on to the Indus plains in what is now Pakistan. A settlement at Mehrgarh is dated from about 8,000/7,000 BC. Almost from the beginning there is evidence of long distance trade in the form of beads of turquoise and lapis lazuli, both apparently imported from northern Afghanistan or central Asia, and of sea shells imported from the Indian Ocean. From before about 5,000 BC the first pottery of baked clay is found. (Even earlier are the first small models of human beings and animals in clay. These in the course of time were to be baked in an oven and turned in time into a long series of terracottas.)

The above indicates the very large number of sites discovered within the extremely wide area of Western Asia, from the Indian Ocean to the Mediterranean. The oldest sites appear to have yielded pottery dated to around 7,500–7,250 BC. It is beyond the scope of this brief survey to postulate with assurance where the pottery was first invented in Western Asia, or whether the invention spread from a single centre of from a number of widely dispersed locations. That there could have been more than one place of origin is supported by the fact that pottery was created separately in at least two more isolated parts of the world – Japan and South America.

On the other hand the technique of combining clay and fire to make cooking pots is simple and easy to communicate. Trade routes provided for the exchange of ideas, as well as of goods and materials, and were often established long before the Neolithic. By attribution to a known source, provenancing studies have traced the prehistoric distribution of rare materials, such as obsidian, over long distances. Pots surely followed, as did the technology of firing pottery.

Fired-clay vessels record the individuality of different production centres, and so establish the 'regionality' referred to by archaeologists. Newly acquired familiarity with the making and use of pottery need not have changed a community's other cultural traits. The sizes, shapes and decoration of pots did not have to be uniform from one territory to another. Local clays would have been used and local tastes followed.

China   More than twenty radiocarbon testing laboratories have been established nationwide and excavations of prehistoric sites are being undertaken over much of China's vast land-mass (An, 1983:1). Late Palaeolithic sites so far dated scientifically are not numerous, with around only twenty radiocarbon dates widely dispersed chrono-logically and spatially (An, 1983:2). This figure is remarkably small when compared with the intensity of archaeological work being conducted in Japan. Twenty Palaeo-lithic dates in China compare with between 2,000 and 4,000 Palaeolithic sites in Japan. (There is controversy, however, between Japanese archaeologists as to whether materials from some sites are firm evidence of human activity.)

By 1988 over 7,000 Neolithic sites spread all over China had been discovered as compared with 150,000 Jomon sites. Over 400 sites had been excavated, and over 1,000 archaeological dates recorded in China (An, 1988:754). In Japan 27,996 excavated Jomon sites were recorded before 1978 (Koyama, 1978:7). Although a great deal of money and time is being devoted to archaeology in China, it is a fraction of Japan's efforts per square kilometre, or per head of the population, or in the total sums of money spent annually.

Material from future finds in China and advances in scientific calculation of dates may quite possibly change present interpretations. Until then, the Chinese dates already recorded provided a current frame for the determination and under-standing of stratigraphical sequences in a number of single sites, and for comparison of cultural periods over the whole country.

Environmentally, China divides into North (including the Huang He – the Yellow River – basin and the steppe region to the north and north-west), and South below a line roughly midway between the Huang He and the Changjiang rivers. The North had temperate, deciduous forests with cultivated millet. The South had subtropical, broadleaf-evergreen forests with cultivated rice. The extreme southern frontiers of China and South-East Asia are tropical.

Some Chinese authorities (An, 1988:755) report that the oldest pottery so far confirmed in China is that found in North China on the Loess tablelands around the basin of the Huang He River, an area often called the cradle of Chinese civilization. While an absolute date of 6,500 BC for this North China pottery is unchallenged, the region and culture which produced the earliest South China pottery are still subject to debate. Some archaeologists claim that very much older pottery, dated before 8,000 BC, has been found in South China. This date remains highly controversial.

North China   The earliest pottery is said to be from four related cultures in North China: the Peiligang in the Xinzheng district in Henan province (illustrations J1a, J1b, J1c), Cishan in Hebei, Dadiwan (also known as the Laoguantai, or as the Baijia culture) in both Shaanxi and Gansu, and Xinglongwa in Inner Mongolia. It has been found in layers below those with pottery and other artefacts of the following Yangshao and later Longshan cultures (An, 1987 and 1988, and personal communication). The date of the Peiligang culture goes back (uncalibrated) to about

5,500–4,950 BC, that of Cishan culture to about 5,405–5,220 BC and that of the Dadiwan culture to about 5,200–4,780 BC. *Peiligang, Cishan and Dadiwan are given a calibrated earliest date no older than 6,500 BC.* The pottery from Xinglongwa 5,290 ± 95 BC (ZK1391), uncalibrated, has been dated about 6,000 BC, calibrated.

Over twenty Peiligang sites, mostly spread over the central Henan region, have already been excavated. From them have come fine smooth and regular stone artefacts that include sole-shaped milling stones on four feet, shovels with two curved ends, and serrated sickles. In addition to this strong circumstantial evidence of agriculture, some storage pits within the houses still contained grain from foxtail and broomcorn millet. Pottery vessels were mainly grey, brown or orange in surface colour and were coil-built. The workmanship was careful and the clay seems to have been refined. Firing was at relatively low temperatures as the sherds are soft and crumbly, and their thickness irregular. The bases of these earliest pots were flat or rounded, but not pointed. Most surfaces were plain but some pieces had comb-impressed line relief or rocker-stamped circles. The range of shapes included spherical jars with two crescent-shaped handles, small-necked jars and shallow bowls on three conical legs (Beijing Museum, 1983:77).

The Cishan, Dadiwan and Xinglongwa cultures had close similarities to Peiligang. Chinese archaeologists are uncertain as to whether the first North China pots were created at one place and the discovery transmitted to the other cultures, or if the invention came independently in each. However, the four cultures existed at approximately the same time and in relative proximity. A single origin appears to be just as possible as multiple origins. Pottery was soon integrated into the developing agricultural life style of the Neolithic age in North China.

On present uncalibrated radiocarbon datings, Peiligang might have commenced pottery making about a hundred years before Cishan. Given the range of statistical error in radiocarbon dates for a period so long ago, this is an insignificant time difference, but the primacy of Peiligang may be supported by another factor. Chinese experts have determined that firing temperatures at Peiligang were about 900°C to 960°C while those at Cishan were from about 700°C to 930°C (An, personal communication). The temperatures at Peiligang probably came from primitive enclosed 'kilns'. (Already one Peiligang kiln site has been discovered.) In contrast, some Cishan vessels would appear to have been fired in open bonfires. As the earliest pots so far discovered at Peiligang seem to have been fired in kilns (the second phase of pottery production) even earlier sherds from Peiligang may still be found. If they are this would confirm Peiligang's primacy with a date earlier than the 6,500 BC quoted above.

South China   The lithic artefacts across the whole south and south-eastern area are similar to and believed to form part of the Hoabinhian tradition. Pottery technology could have been closely related throughout the rather homogeneous southern ecological and cultural expanse including its peripheries. Coarse pottery found at Xianrendong, Zengpiyan, Baozitou and other sites, is said by some to be as much as about 2,000 years earlier than the earliest of North China, but these earliest South China datings are rejected by other archaeologists.

The conflicting views on the age of the first South China pottery have been expressed frequently and at length by K.C. (Kwang-chi) Chang, who argues that very early figures are correct, and An Zhimin, who disagrees.

This clash of opinions between experts illustrates the continuing controversy over the reliability of absolute dating methods, particularly for radiocarbon. Both men are recognized authorities on Chinese prehistory – An Zhimin of the Institute of Archaeology in Beijing, and K.C. Chang a professor of archaeology at Harvard University. The opposing statements of the two authorities were on one occasion printed in the same book, *7,000 Years of Chinese Civilization* (1983). In that book (pages 32, 33, italics added) Chang wrote:

> Sites scattered in South China, some in limestone caves and others along riverbanks or seacoasts are loosely unified by a coarse pottery often impressed with cord marks. A series of radiocarbon dates place these sites into the interval of *approximately 10,000–5,000 BC*, which make these pottery remains the earliest known so far in China. The best known of these sites are those in the limestone caves of Xianrendong in Wannian, Jiangxi in central Yangtze, and Zengpiyan in Guilin, Guangxi, in the karst hills of the southwest . . . A different neolithic culture is found in archaeological remains in the north.

The editors (including An Zhimin) of the Beijing Museum of Chinese History wrote in the same book (pages 10, 12):

> Starting from 7,000–8,000 years ago (5,000–6,000 BC), after a slow process of development, a large number of communities dwelling in villages made their appearance in the valley of the Yellow River and to the south and north of the Yangzijiang. [Author: these Yangzijiang sites are a somewhat vague reference to the South China sites in question.] The forefathers of the Chinese nation began to cultivate cereals, to breed domestic animals, to make use of smoothed stone tools and to master the technology of pottery. In this way the Neolithic Age began.
>
> Belonging to the Peiligang culture, located in Peiligang in the Xinzheng District, in the Henan Province, are the earliest cultural remains of the Neolithic Period of the Central Plain. These finds, which date back to more than 7,000 years ago, present evident primitive traits. In that period both agriculture and animal husbandry had already achieved a certain level of development. Within the ambit of the cultural succession of ancient China the Peiligang Culture presents close ties with the Yangshao Culture, of which it is the precursor.

In a separate article An Zhimin (1983:4) referred more directly to the southern sites:

> The C14 date for shell from the upper layer of the Xianrendong site, in Wan-

nien Prefecture in Guangxi, is 8,920 ± 240 BC, nearly 2,000 years older than the date (6,875 ± 180 BC) for the bone from the lower layer of the same site. Again, the C14 date of shell (9,360 ± 180 BC) from the Zengpiyan site, Kuei-lin city, Guangxi, is inconsistent with the date of bone (5,630 ± 410 BC) by 3,000 years, and with the date of charcoal (4,000 ± 90 BC) from the same layer by over 5,000 years. A problem is clearly involved in the dating of the shell, and most likely it is older contamination derived from the carboniferous underground water. A series of experiments revealed that the shell samples from this area generally give by 1,000 to 2,000 years older dates.

Chang has written more recently (1986):

> The apparent great antiquity of the Southern Chinese cave pottery to this date is faced with much scepticism from leading archaeologists, who believe that radiocarbon samples recovered from a limestone environment must have been somehow contaminated (An Zhimin, 1984). But an extensive series of experiments with samples collected from a variety of limestone environments by the physicists of the radiocarbon laboratories at both the Institute of Archaeology and Peking University have show no consistent pattern of deviation from samples collected elsewhere (Kaogu Xuebao, 1982:243–50), and the early dating of the Zengpiyan site is confirmed by the thermoluminescence technique, which has resulted in twelve dates ranging from 7,160 ± 930 BP to 10,370 ± 870 BP, approximately the same range as the radiocarbon samples (W.T. Wang – Kaoguxue Jikan, 1984:321–7). As of now we must say that Zengpiyan pottery is the earliest found in China so far. That does not, however, suggest that pottery was 'diffused' from South China to North China, even though the earliest pottery yet found from Peiligang is dated two millennia later. In this age of discovery, especially with regard to the early postglacial, every new find can open up new vistas on the ancient cultural-historical scene, and the game of who–is–earlier or who–gives–who–receives cannot be played for at least another ten years.
>
> The same early age was again detected in samples from an open–air site, Baozitou in Nan–ning, Guangxi, which is on a river terrace and has nothing to do with limestone caves. A series of shell–midden sites (including Baozitou) was found in the 1960s and early 1970s along the Yung–chiang River, and these sites yielded human burials and artifacts of the same range and similar kinds as those found in the caves.

Of South China pottery from non-limestone areas, An has written more recently (1988, personal communication):

> The sites near the shore of Lake Donting are almost contemporary with the Peiligang culture in North China, Zaoshi in Hunan has been dated 6,000–5,200 BC.

Additionally, An (personal communication, 1988) reconfirmed his stand against the much earlier datings of South China pottery:

> In the limestone areas of South China (and also of Southeastern Asia), there is often a big margin of error in C14 dating, especially for shell specimens, which usually cause dates to be attributed to a period more than 1,000 years earlier. Therefore the C14 dates of this region can't be taken as completely reliable. For example, two specimens from Dalongtan in Liuzhou City of Guangxi Province have been C14 dated for $21,380 \pm 250$ BC (BK82091) and $19,480 \pm$ BC (PV379–2), but they are obviously too early for specimens found in associations with fragments of pottery, so the dates can't be believed.

Even more recently An has published a paper, 'Application of carbon-14 dating to the Early Neolithic in South China' (1989), which maintains his rejection of the earliest dates for pottery in South China.

It is very probable that older Chinese pottery will be discovered but, on present findings, it is difficult to reconcile the controversial South China datings with those accepted for North China. Although China extends over a tremendous area, hunter-gatherers probably traded over long distances, as did the emerging agricultural cultures. Once the pottery-making technique had been invented and found useful, it was so simple that it is hard to believe that it would not have been transmitted far and wide overland within centuries rather than thousands of years.

The above amply demonstrates that a clash of opinion over the interpretation of carbon-14 tests can persist for years without any sign of reconciliation. It follows that to establish dates for the earliest pottery is a hazardous business. Not surprisingly, some recent art-historian authors have stood well back from the problem.

The controversy over very early dates for South China pottery has not been mentioned by Valenstein in the revised edition of her carefully researched *Handbook of Chinese Ceramics* (1989: 10, 16/18). She includes no pottery earlier than that of Peiligang and Cishan of North China.

More recently Vainker's *Chinese Pottery and Porcelain* (1991), for the British Museum, gives three different statements as to the earliest pottery dates in China. These are on a diminishing scale from 9,000 to 7,000 to 6,500 BC (pages 10, 14 and 226).

Siberia

At the time of this writing, explicit dating and details of the earliest pottery in Siberia and other parts of the former Soviet Union are not readily available. Professor Dobrinsky of the Institute of Archaeology, Moscow (personal communication, October, 1990) has written that, according to his knowledge, the oldest pottery found in the Soviet Union is not more ancient than the sixth to fifth millennium BC. However, in 1990, A.P. Derev'anko published his *Palaeolithic of North Asia and the Problem of Ancient Migrations*. He reported a small number of sherds found in Siberia at the sites of Barkasnaya III and Ust'-Ul'ma II, on the Selemdga River, a tributary of the Zeya River, which joins the Amur River a good way upstream from Khabarovsk. These sherds were found with microcores in a stratum believed to be older than 10,000–8,500 BC on geological bases. He also reported ceramic sherds dated 'on coal' of $10,960 \pm 120$ years BC (LE 1781) at the Gas'a Settlement in Sakachi-Al'an on the Amur river about sixty kilometres downstream from Khabarovsk.

Around the tenth millennium BC pottery-making was widespread in central and south-western Japan, where the population was relatively dense reflecting adequate food supplies close to small settlements. Further north, the colder climate in Siberia and Japan's northern island of Hokkaido was far less conducive to pottery-making. The few recently reported finds in Siberia are hard to account for. These few sherds are claimed by one archaeologist to be contemporary with those which have been excavated from sites all over Japan, *except* Hokkaido, which is nearest to Siberia. The first evidence of pottery in Hokkaido was four thousand years away.

It is not unknown in all regions and at all times for an invention to be made, to fail to gain widespread acceptance, and to fall by the wayside. This would seem to have occurred with ceramics in Siberia, that is if these recently announced dates can be accepted. There is no evidence of any further sherd being found there until the sixth millennium, shortly after pottery-making had reached Hokkaido from the south. In the light of the very limited evidence available from the Russian reports, the most one can say is that if the dating is accurate than these early Siberian ceramics formed a very short-lived phase. Further, there appears to be no unambiguous statement that the sherds are of pots rather than ceramic figurines.

Korea

Korea was settled during the Palaeolithic age and stone-tool techniques were linked with those of North China and later Siberia to the north, as is evidenced by the characteristic wedge core. In those very early days a land-bridge could also have served in transmission between Korea and Japan. The Korean peninsula is believed to have become a no-man's land after the end of the Pleistocene as the Palaeolithic population appears to have migrated north leaving a cultural hiatus of over a millennium (Kim, 1986:29), until a Neothlithic culture developed from about 6,000 BC to 4,500 BC (Im, 1987:801).[2] The earliest Korean pottery is dated no earlier than 6,000 BC.

Most of today's Japanese believe that pottery did not originate in Japan but was first imported from Korea, or China or Siberia. There is no evidence to support the assumption. There have been notable pottery imports from Korea to Japan over the last 2,500 years, but not earlier. The first unglazed earthenware vessels made in Korea were not unlike pots being made in Japan, but this was about 4,000 or more years after Japan had begun to make pottery.

The earliest production of pottery in Korea seems to have been after the earliest in China, but there is no evidence that pottery came from China before production had been well established in Korea. The Chinese styles were very different from the

Korean. On the other hand, early comb-pattern Korean pottery shows considerable similarity to contemporary pottery in Japan.

The sites that have yielded the earliest pottery so far found in Korea are at present believed to be on the East coast at Osan-ri and Sop'ohang. They lie further north than Tongsam-dong which has yielded somewhat younger pottery. Links between Tongsam-dong and Kyushu in the south are clearly evidenced. A more northern contact with Japan is possible but not yet verified. Although pottery was being made in Japan thousands of years before Korea, there could have been independent invention in Korea.

MAPS

Key to Map 1:   Modern and Ancient 'Prefecture' (Ken) Names

	Modern	*Ancient*		*Modern*	*Ancient*
1	Hokkaido	Ezo	27	Osaka	(a) Izumi
2	Aomori	Mutsu (or Michinoku)			(b) Settsu
3	Akita	Ugo			(c) Kawachi
4	Iwate	Rikuchû	28	Kyoto	(a) Tango
5	Yamagata	Uzen			(b) Tanba
6	Miyagi	Rikuzen			(c) Yamashiro
7	Fukushima	(a) Iwashiro	29	Nara	Yamato
		(b) Iwaki	30	Hyogo	(a) Tajima
8	Gumma	Kamizuke			(b) Harima
9	Tochigi	Shimozuke	31	Okayama	(a) Mimasaka
10	Ibaragi	Hitachi			(b) Bicchu
11	Saitama	} Musashi			(c) Bizen
12	Tokyo				
13	Chiba	(a) Shimosa	32	Hiroshima	(a) Aki
		(b) Kazusa			(b) Bingo
		(c) Awa			(c) Bicchu
14	Kanagawa	Sagami	33	Tottori	(a) Hôki
15	Niigata	Echigo			(b) Inaba
16	Nagano	Shinano	34	Shimane	(a) Iwami
17	Yamanashi	Kahi			(b) Izumo
18	Shizuoka	(a) Tôtomi	35	Yamaguchi	(a) Nagato
		(b) Suruga			(b) Suhô
19	Aichi	(a) Owari	36	Kagawa	Sanuki
		(b) Mikawa	37	Tokushima	Awa
20	Gifu	(a) Mino	38	Kochi	Tosa
		(b) Hida	39	Ehime	Iyo
21	Toyama	Ecchu	40	Fukuoka	(a) Chikuzen
22	Ishikawa	(a) Kaga			(b) Buzen
		(b) Noto			(c) Chikugo
23	Fukui	Echizen	41	Saga	} Hizen
			42	Nagasaki	
24	Shiga	Ohmi	43	Ohita	Bungo
25	Mie	(a) Iga	44	Kumamoto	Higo
		(b) Ise	45	Miyazaki	Hûga
		(c) Shima	46	Kagoshima	(a) Satsuma
26	Wakayama	Kii			(b) Ohsumi
			47	Okinawa	Ryukyu

Maps

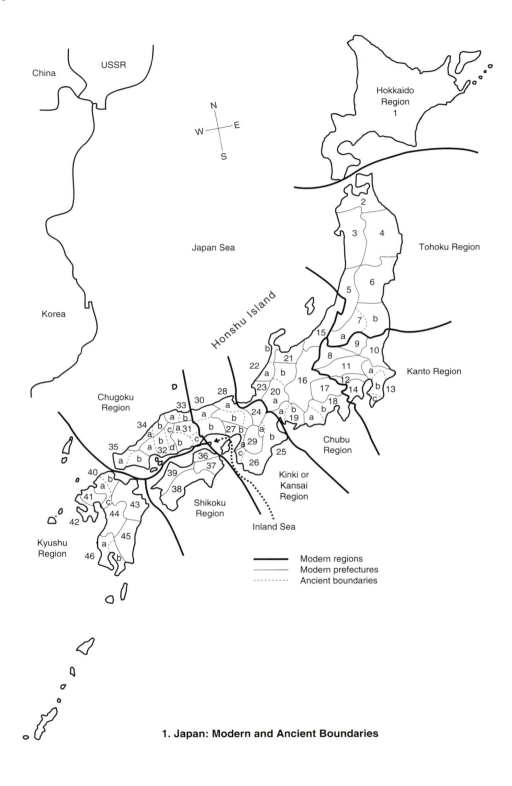

1. Japan: Modern and Ancient Boundaries

16

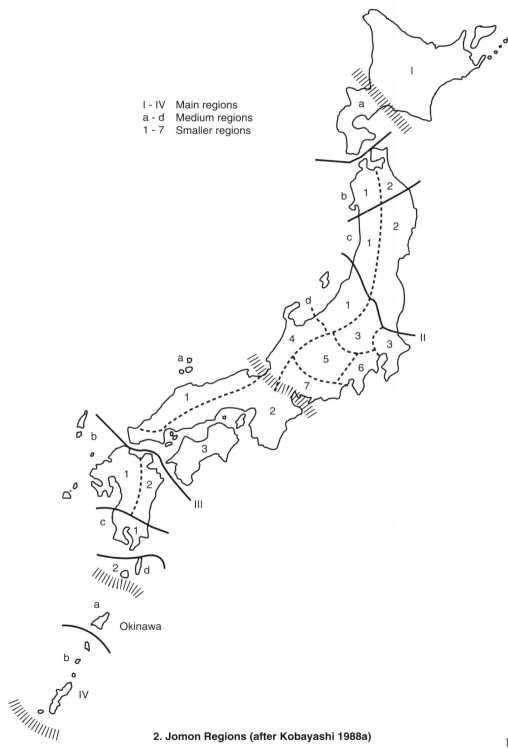

I - IV   Main regions
a - d   Medium regions
1 - 7   Smaller regions

Okinawa

2. Jomon Regions (after Kobayashi 1988a)

17

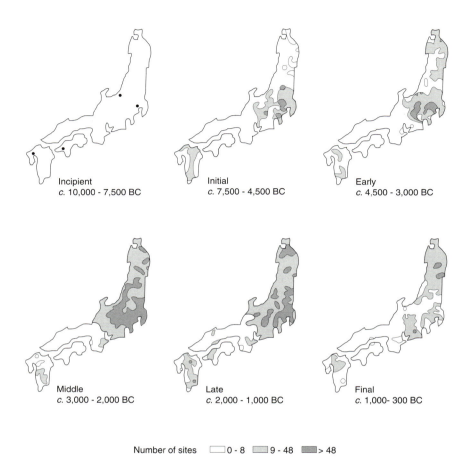

Incipient
c. 10,000 - 7,500 BC

Initial
c. 7,500 - 4,500 BC

Early
c. 4,500 - 3,000 BC

Middle
c. 3,000 - 2,000 BC

Late
c. 2,000 - 1,000 BC

Final
c. 1,000- 300 BC

Number of sites ☐ 0 - 8 ▨ 9 - 48 ▨ > 48

3. Distribution of Jomon Sites (after Koyama 1978:481)

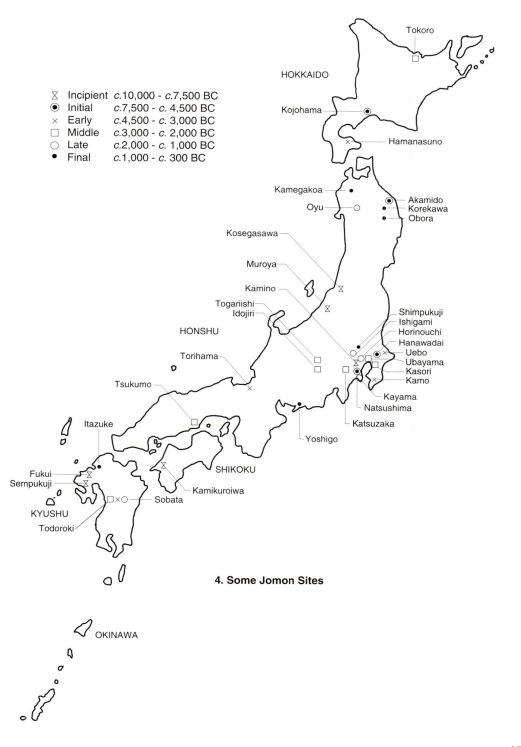

⋈	Incipient	*c.*10,000 - *c.*7,500 BC
⊙	Initial	*c.*7,500 - *c.* 4,500 BC
×	Early	*c.*4,500 - *c.* 3,000 BC
□	Middle	*c.*3,000 - *c.* 2,000 BC
○	Late	*c.*2,000 - *c.* 1,000 BC
●	Final	*c.*1,000 - *c.* 300 BC

4. Some Jomon Sites

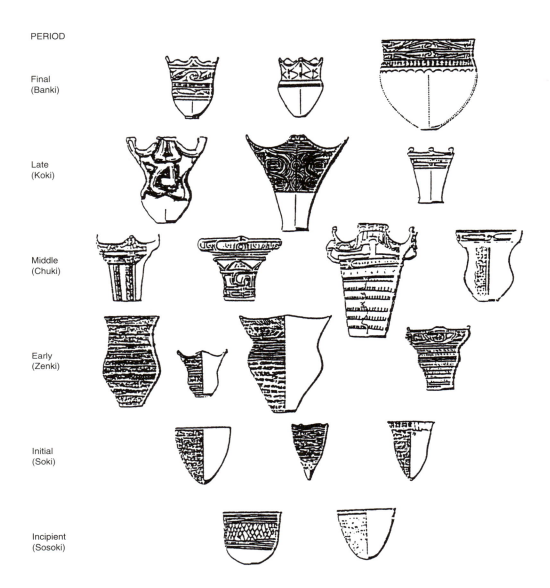

PERIOD

Final
(Banki)

Late
(Koki)

Middle
(Chuki)

Early
(Zenki)

Initial
(Soki)

Incipient
(Sosoki)

5. Typical Jomon Jars – Kanto Region

Selected and drawn by Kenji Fukuda. Names of periods in brackets are Japanese language equivalents.

Jomon Pottery

Phases

The invention of fireproof pottery around 10,000 BC is the milestone which marks the beginning of the Jomon period.

In 1877 an American, Edward Sylvester Morse, found unglazed earthenware pots in a shell-mound at Omori beside the railway track between Tokyo and Yokohama. He labelled them, from their predominant decorative motif, 'cord-marked' and this was later translated as 'Jomon'. The people who made the Jomon pottery, a forest-adapted, hunting, gathering and fishing culture, are now also referred to as Jomon.

In 1937 the brilliant pioneer Sugao Yamanouchi had only fifty reported Jomon types to work with, all from the Tohoku and Kanto regions. On the assumption that the pottery from other parts of Japan would correspond with those already reported, he constructed sequences of types and aligned them into five sub-periods, ten types to each with pottery groups representing 'phases'. Yamanouchi initiated a convention, which is still accepted by Japanese archaeologists, of dividing the Jomon period into phases.

Until the beginning of the 1950s the earliest pottery in Japan was thought to have been made about 2,500 BC, a theory based on comparisons with pottery from near Lake Baikal in Siberia, and from Denmark. Unfortunately, these continental wares were themselves either not securely dated or not comparable. Since the 1950s scientific methods of dating have revealed that Jomon pottery began much earlier than had previously been believed. Radiocarbon dating of materials from the Natsushima shell-mound at Yokosuka near Yokohama gave ages in excess of 7,000 BC. Since then, tests of hundreds of specimens from excavations of the strata in, or above, or below which Jomon pottery has been found, have reduced the possibility of extreme error in dating (Keally and Muto, 1982:246/275). These tests have changed the picture dramatically. The first vessels are now generally believed to have been produced from about 10,000 BC or even earlier.

In the 1960s with the excavation of more and more early pottery, Yamanouchi's phases were increased by one to encompass pottery much older than that found at Natsushima shell-mound. A majority of archaeologists now accepts six phases, a convention originated in 1961 by Yamanouchi and established in the English language by Kidder in 1968. The new scientific datings have extended the chronology but made little change in Yamanouchi's original sequences.

In Japanese the original five phases were named by Yamanouchi as Soki, Zenki, Chuki, Koki and Banki. These were aptly translated into English as Earliest, Early, Middle, Late and Latest, and firmly established in the 1950s by Kidder's usage in several publications. When, in the 1960s, discovery of even older sites created the need for a sixth phase, this was named in Japanese as Sosoki. However, in English this promptly raised the question of what could possibly predate Earliest? Even worse, how could the name Earliest continue now that a preceding phase had been established?

In order to preserve the meaning of what was already in the literature, and to prevent disruption and confusion, the name Sub-earliest was proposed by Kidder. Despite its good intentions the term was not generally adopted. Other Japanese archaeologists have called it either 'Incipient Jomon' or 'Pre-Jomon, or 'Proto-Jomon'. Years later, the Early, Middle and Late core of the sequence has stood the test of time, but the outer phases have been renamed. A degree of consensus has gradually emerged. This book follows the six phase names used by Tsuboi, Kato, Kobayashi and others: Incipient, Initial, Early, Middle, Late and Final.

Western scholars tend to define their terms (and pottery types) very precisely and to make these definitions clear to their readers. Their Japanese opposite numbers tend to prefer imprecisely defined expressions which avoid the concept and importance of scientific precision. Consequently inconsistencies are common when pots are said to be of a certain phase without the writer, or speaker, mentioning what calendar time range he has in mind for his terminology. The same pottery type, and even the same pot, is sometimes put into different phases by different archaeologists. (This may sometimes be justified by regional overlaps going beyond accepted phase datings.)

Even today dates based on radiocarbon and other physical tests are still not accepted by a few Japanese archaeologists. This minority is small and dwindling but it is advisable to repeat what Kiyotari Tsuboi (1977:192/194) has written:

> There is strong disagreement among scholars concerning the date of the beginning of the Jomon period. The majority have established for the beginning of the Incipient Jomon the date 10,000 BC ... The minority group believes the origins of pottery fall somewhere much closer to 2,500 BC ... The minority's dates contradict not only the various laboratory measurements, but also geological and palaeoclimatological data that support the older dates.[3]

The 2,500 BC beginning date allocated by archaeologists working without the benefit of laboratory testing methods may now be treated as only of historical interest. It is mentioned here because the old 'short chronology' is still assumed to be valid in at least one recent book in English (Nishimura 1986).

Of greater significance, the Jomon period and its six phases are still not clarified into a single series of phase dates accepted by all archaeologists. All date indications for the beginning and ending of Jomon phases are approximations that may be modified later in the light of further research and discoveries. Substantive typological and regional time-overlaps blur rigid divisions but agreement on a temporal framework must be attempted even though earlier types may have continued to be made in later phases. Conversely, there may have been prototypes in some regions of types designated to later phases elsewhere. Regional overlaps in phase datings must be accepted like tolerances in time dates. Table 1 gives rounded-off, average dates now used by a small majority of Japanese archaeologists. A sample range of Jomon dates has been compiled from Keally and Muto in 'Jomon Jidai no nendai' (1982:246/275), as given in Endnote 4.[4]

Table 1 Jomon Phases

Incipient	(Sosoki)	10,000–7,500 BC
Initial	(Soki)	7,500–4,500 BC
Early	(Zenki)	4,500–3,000 BC
Middle	(Chuki)	3,000–2,000 BC
Late	(Koki)	2,000–1,000 BC
Final	(Banki)	1,000– 300 BC

Whether to use 10,000 BC or 10,500 BC is a small difference for the beginning of the time series. It is accepted that some sherds appear to be older than 10,000 BC but these sherds are often fragmentary, different testing methods give wide discrepancies, and tolerances are often very large. A round figure of 10,000 BC seems advisable until testing measurements are more accurate.

The phase dates given in the above table are less contentious for the Early, Middle, Late and Final phases, but this does not ensure unanimity in English language publications. There is no unanimity on where to draw the lines between successive pottery phases.[5]

The dividing line between the termination of the Incipient Jomon phase and the commencement of the Initial phase is still a subject of controversy. The 8,000 BC date given by some archaeologists compares with 7,000 BC used by others. Cord-marking appeared from about 7,500 BC. This appears to be a useful date to terminate the Incipient and begin the Initial phase. It is given by rather more than half of Japanese archaeologists and ceramicists who choose to include cord-marked vessels in the Initial phase. They regard the cord-marked Yoriitomon style, the first pottery style to be found in relative abundance, and typified by vessels from the Natsushima shell-mound (black and white illustration J6), as an identifying style of the Initial phase.

The Initial phase is prominent in the archaeological record because of its shell-mounds, particularly those in the Kanto region, where pottery first became common, and a little later those in the Tohoku region further north. The rivers and seas, particularly along the east side of the Japanese islands, were very well stocked. Shell-mounds show clearly a growing reliance on shellfish and fishing as supplements to hunting and gathering. These rubbish heaps, which have survived over the millennia, enclose within the piles of shells other refuse such as broken pottery, stone tools, and various animal bones.

As well as the introduction of cord-marking, the distinction between the Incipient and Initial phases is shown in other developments. Palaeolithic features were disappearing and there is increasing evidence of arrowheads.

Other new objects included fish-hooks for inner-bay fishing, found for example in Natsushima shell-mound.

Regions within Japan

Just as the ten millennia of the Jomon period have to be divided into phases to make its evolution comprehensible, so also must Japan be divided into regions if the development of pottery styles is to be understood.

Although the overall population grew substantially over time, some regional concentrations grew as others declined. However, the strong regional character of the Jomon culture shows a general continuity throughout the period, and the stability of the regional demarcations is seen as evidence that these hunger-gatherers were not given to migration.

Japan is a collection of islands lying between latitudes 46 and 26 degrees north. A casual look at a map of Japan may lead some of us to think of north and south relationships, but the Japanese refer more often to the spread from east to west. A more accurate term, north-east/south-west, is rarely used. The four main islands are: Hokkaido in the north; Honshu, the main central island (which curves west as it extends southward); Shikoku, close to Honshu and just off its south coast; and Kyushu, in the south-west. The Okinawa group of smaller islands lies further south.

The earliest pottery is found on three of Japan's main islands (Kyushu, Shikoku and Honshu). Sites with later Jomon pottery are widely scattered not only over all the main islands but also on the small Izu islands off Tokyo, on small islands off the coast of Kyushu, and as far south as the main island of Okinawa.

Within the main islands the regional boundaries have arisen from natural barriers to population movement. Extensive mountain ranges, rivers and lakes have created distinct areas, which even within living memory have preserved cultural differences. Some of these differences stem from the wide latitudinal span of Japan's archipelago, which provides a climate varying from the sub-tropical to the sub-arctic. It naturally follows that these climatic differences generate contrasting zones of vegetation.

A further factor is that there were climatic changes during the Jomon millennia, and these long-term changes affected all regions.

From this complicated picture it is only necessary for our purposes to emphasize the division between the warm-temperate forest of broadleaf evergreen trees, and the cool-temperate deciduous forest further north. This environmental split between two major habitats was of special importance to the Jomon hunter-gatherers, and it roughly corresponds to the split into two main pottery regions as described in the following paragraphs.

Nowadays, although Japan is small, it is customarily broken into nine regions. These are, from the north-east to the south-west: Hokkaido; Tohoku; Kanto; Chubu; Kinki (or Kansai); Chugoku; Shikoku; Kyushu; and Okinawa. The regions are subdivided into prefectures for which, in this book, the Japanese equivalent, 'ken', will be used.

Tatsuo Kobayashi, with his intimate knowledge of Jomon pottery styles, suggests that the standard nine regions can be compressed into two main pottery regions each with distinctive sub-regions and sub-sub-regions. He has drawn the locations of all the major types of the entire Jomon period on a series of maps. To visualize and compare areas of production during the whole of the Jomon period, he overlaid the maps and observed remarkably similar regional demarcations which varied little down the ages. These he has shown on a single map (see Map 2 above, p. 17). Kobayashi's two main regions are created by dividing the whole of Japan by a line running across the geographic waistline of the main island, Honshu. (This line may be seen in the centre of Map 2, and runs north-west from a point near the modern city of Nagoya.)

In discussing the entire Jomon period, the country is frequently referred to as either 'Western Japan' or 'Eastern Japan', a climatic divide which closely approximates to Kobayashi's two pottery regions. Cultural and demographic development was very different between the West with its broadleaf evergreen forests, and the East with its deciduous trees. The Japanese concept of their East/West (rather than North/South) divide is a national tradition often referred to by Japanese archaeologists and environmentalists. Western Japan incorporates the West Honshu regions, Chugoku and Kansai, together with west and south the islands of Shikoku and Kyushu. Eastern Japan comprises Hokkaido and the rest of Honshu-Chubu, the Kanto and Tohoku regions.

Today's regional and prefectural (ken) boundaries differ little from Kobayashi's concept but there were no names in the Jomon period. Today's names are used in this text to aid in locating Jomon sites on modern maps (see key to Map 1 above, p. 15).

One other name, 'Central Japan' (or 'Central Honshu') is also employed frequently. Japanese archaeologists define the 'central' area as being the Chubu and Kanto regions of Eastern Japan.

Population and Environment

Incipient Phase (*c.* 10,000–7,500 BC)

Although more dense than in most other parts of the world at that time, the Jomon population density was extremely low and at first habitations were not in close proximity. The hunter-gatherers do not appear to have organized into tribal group-ings. Transmission of the pottery-making techniques from place to place would have been retarded, but not prevented, by long distances, high mountains and wide rivers. Japan is not a vast country (it is roughly the size of Britain) but sites were widely dispersed. One of the oldest sites, Odai-Yamamoto in the north of Honshu, is about 2,000 kilometres overland from Sempukuji in Kyushu. Over the entire area from Kyushu and Shikoku to the Kanto and Tohoku regions, most Incipient phase vessels have such similar traits that it is entirely possible that the first pottery-making started in a single centre and then dispersed. Pottery-making techniques could have passed from one household to another, although of course long-distance transmission could have taken hundreds of years.

Their cooking pots were the products of individuals working in their spare time to make vessels which extended their families' choice of food from the raw and the baked to include the boiled. For thousands of years the only vessels were jars for cooking. The Incipient Jomon economy was, and remained, based on hunting and gathering, but the creation of cooking vessels is seen by archaeologists as a major factor in the adoption of sedentary life. We can only guess what kind of food went into the first Jomon pots although we do have a fair knowledge of what resources were being exploited. Studies of hunter-gatherers past and present show that the late winter and early spring period is always a critical time for food. No doubt the spring growth of bamboo shoots from the underground rootstock was as keenly sought after in prehistory as it is today. These shoots need long boiling to be digestible, so the first hunter-gatherer to make pottery could have been prompted by the urge to turn tough vegetables into food. Any combination of plants, nuts, tubers, meat, fish and shellfish could soon have followed.

Fishing played a significant role in almost all hunter-gatherer cultures world-wide. In Japan the Jomon people lived on the islands of their archipelago surrounded by seas stocked with fish. For many of them fishing and the gathering of shellfish were of increasing importance.

Although early evidence of settlement at the coast has disappeared beneath the sea levels of today, the evidence of later phases suggests that even during the Incipient many of the Jomon were coastal people. As fish became a staple part of the Jomon diet, so fishing technology developed to satisfy this new emphasis.

Initial Phase (*c. 7,500–4,500 BC*)

The population in northern Honshu (the Tohoku region) was still sparse and scattered with weak concentrations; Central Honshu was already covered extensively; Western Japan, except around the Inland Sea area between Honshu and Shikoku, was virtually unoccupied; but Kyushu was well populated (Koyama 1978:47, 49). (Map 4 gives site distribution in this and the following phases.)

Early Phase (*c.* 4,500–3,000 BC)

From the beginning of the Early phase, the Jomon culture became more dynamic and complex as it adapted to changing forests and a warmer environment. In Eastern Japan sites became more common and larger, pottery more abundant. An expanding fishing economy and the accompanying increase in the coastal population from the Kanto north to southern Hokkaido were marked by the growing number of large shell-mounds created on well selected locations around bays and estuaries, and occasionally along rivers. Many pit-dwellings increased in size and reveal potsherds at every site. (Pit-dwellings were houses with floors dug a little below the surrounding surface level.) More permanent and semi-permanent settlements appeared. In the Tohoku and Central Japan regions settlements merged and spread. Population growth accelerated except in Western Honshu where the sparse population declined. In Kyushu a widely scattered Initial Jomon occupation separated during Early and Middle Jomon into two clusters with a tendency to proliferation in eastern Kyushu and contraction in the west (Koyama, 1978:49).

Following the marine transgression of around 4,000 BC, when the sea rose above today's levels and indented the coastline, an increasing number of shell-mounds show that the plentiful resources of the sea were more fully exploited. Initial and Early Jomon, Kanto-style sherds excavated on Oshima, an island about 27 kilometres from the coast of Tokyo Bay, give evidence of movement by sea. Beyond Oshima, at least as far as Miyakejima, others of the Izu group of seven islands extend for a distance of about 290 kilometres south from the entrance to Tokyo Bay. Sherds, possibly of Early Jomon, have been excavated on the southernmost island of the group, Hachijojima. Six paddles and the remains of a dug-out canoe from the Kamo site, in the Kanto region (near the tip of the Chiba peninsula about 70 kilometres south of Tokyo), and similar artefacts from several other sites around the country, give more direct evidence of marine transport.

Middle Phase (*c.* 3,000–2,000 BC)

The climate, which had reached its warmest during the Early Jomon phase, was cooling but still warmer than today. The temperate deciduous mixed forests of Eastern Japan were probably at their richest with nuts, deer and boar plentiful. In contrast, the evergreen broadleaf forests of Western Japan seem not to have been so bountiful.

As in the Initial and Early phases, coastal and river-fishing settlements continued making pottery, which had become a major feature of the hunter-gatherer-fisher economy. Additionally, during Middle Jomon the inland areas of Central Honshu recorded spectacular growth in pottery production, together with bold innovations in decoration. This vigour was most powerfully expressed by the expanding populations of the mountain valleys and plateaux of Nagano and Niigata prefectures in the Chubu region.

Particularly in the Chubu and adjacent Kanto region of Central Japan, the Middle Jomon population reached a peak. Shuzo Koyama (1978:56) estimates the inhabitants of Japan to have been 21,900 during Initial Jomon, rising to 262,500 in Middle Jomon. Koyama bases his estimates on the number and size of all known sites combined with a study of environmental conditions and exploitation patterns to gauge the efficiency of subsistence. Other archaeologists give different figures, but Koyama's calculations for the Middle Jomon appear to be reasonable when related to the area of rich forests available for Jomon foragers, particularly in Eastern Japan, and to the wealth of Middle Jomon pottery that has been discovered.

Middle Jomon rectangular houses had an average floor space of about 16 square metres, and square ones about 12 square metres. Round houses also appeared of about the same size. All may have housed from four to possibly more than eight occupants. The houses had deep post-holes and central fireplaces which has made locating the dwellings relatively easy, but the construction of these rather elaborate houses caused displacement and erased much evidence of earlier occupation (Kidder, 1983).

With the denser population and greater availability of food, particularly in Central Honshu, living habits changed and much time was devoted to making more pottery with increasingly elaborate decoration. This happy state of affairs continued for most of the Middle phase, but towards the end the cooling climate seems to have seriously affected the mountain communities of Central Honshu. Their population levels declined swiftly and dramatically. The reasons for this are still not clear, but lower temperatures might have reduced available plant foods, some of which might possibly have been cultivated.

Late Jomon (*c.* 2,000–1,000 BC)

During these one thousand years of a cooler climate, the overall population became lower, in some areas much lower than during Middle Jomon. The size of settlements seems generally to have been smaller and usually with less pottery per dwelling. However, there were clusters of medium density and contact between communities did not appear to lessen. During this phase pottery vessels from all parts of the country came to resemble each other more closely in the range of their shapes, and also possibly in their range of functions.

During Middle Jomon, shell-mounds had been mostly concentrated on the Kanto coastline, especially around Tokyo Bay, but these were left stranded when the sea retreated to its present level during the Late Jomon phase. Then the concentration moved north to the Tohoku region around Sendai Bay. Elsewhere shell-mounds were widely scattered.

Dependence on coastal fishing and shellfish collecting continued to grow during Late Jomon. Kanto fishing seems to have relied on nets and, probably, traps.

Tohoku fishing seems to have been much more advanced and complex. There fish-hooks, toggle harpoons, fish-spears and the like for coastal and open-sea fishing were especially centered in Iwate-ken. New kinds of fishing equipment and tools found in the shell-mounds there are surprising in their variety.

Final Phase (*c.* 1,000–300 BC)

Population in all Japan fell from the peak of about 262,500 in the Middle phase to about 161,500 in the Final (Koyama, 1978:56). Except in the Tohoku region, site numbers declined drastically. The Kanto and Chubu regions remained relatively densely occupied but even there the decrease in site numbers was dramatic (Koyama, 1978:50).

The Cultivation Controversy

Some sites have given evidence thought to indicate some sort of plant-tending and a few archaeologists use terms like 'shifting agriculture' (slash and burn), 'plant-manipulation', and 'vegeculture'.[6] In inland sites in the Chubu region during Middle Jomon, the presence of hoe-like tools of sandstone and shale (usually called chip-stone-axes, but too soft to cut trees) points to their use to dig roots. A long, edible tuber, still eaten and now named nagaimo (long potato), could have supplemented other foods from gathering and the chase.

However, recent study with scanning electron microscopes (by Akiko Matsutani in 1987) has shown that seeds from Chubu sites thought to have been of domesticated plants are, in fact, of wild plants. Moreover most biologists feel that the forests of Eastern Japan yielded more than enough in wild foods to make cultivation far more work than foraging, and therefore unlikely. However, although not yet confirmed, some recent discoveries suggest that from the Early phase (or even the Initial) some Jomon were planting and tending gourds and beans. Tatsuo Kobayashi feels that the Jomon use of nearly every species of available plants and animals suggests a conscious and rational use of nature's bounty with a low-level use of less desired species to avoid depletion of preferred ones. He calls this 'unfenced ranching'. Although the weight of opinion these days seems to lean against 'farming', few specialists rule out some sort of 'tending', such as self-imposed restraints on hunting, or clearing under oak trees to make it easier to collect acorns, or even weeding out trees that did not produce nuts.

Pottery at Burials

During the whole Jomon period, no elaborate tombs or burial chambers were built, but some jars were associated with interment. Burial practices seem to have taken a wide variety of styles only partially relate to sex, or to age, or to status. There does not appear to be any study yet made that describes all Jomon burial-jar styles by regions and temporal variations, other than a very old one by Makoto Watanabe. Although in the Kanto region during Middle Jomon much evidence suggests burials in the centre of villages, some interment of adults was probably on the outskirts of settlements where few pottery jars have yet been found. Some children were buried in jars individually, in or near houses. (A Late phase Horinouchi-type jar (illustration J74) contained bones thought to be those of a new-born child.) Small jars buried usually in the south-west part of the floors of many dwellings in the Chubu and Kanto regions are likely to have contained human placenta. Secondary burial of cleaned bones appears to have been common.

The surrounding shells have helped preserve some human bones in burial vessels recovered from shell-mounds, but the acid in most of Japan's soil dissolved bones over the years. The results of phosphate tests of jars' contents have left room for conjecture. Jars still containing bones at the time of excavation are rare until the Late and Final Jomon phases when they become more common.

Identification of vessels as burial jars is difficult. Those for interments cannot be distinguished visually from household jars. Some jars without human remains seem to have been included in the burials. It appears that most jars, if not all, had been used for other purposes before fulfilling their final function. Some jars are found buried upside down, a practice which has not been found everywhere, but seems to indicate that jars buried this way were for interments. Nature has broken most jars since they were buried, but some have been found with a hole bored in their bases (illustration J58). The holes were perhaps intended to enable a spirit to escape, or to discourage re-use by a scavenger.

Pottery Techniques

Incipient Phase (*c.* 10,000–7,500 BC)

The Jomon achievement was to find that, when they moulded clay and fired it, they had a vessel which held water and did not return to the plasticity of the original clay. The Jomon peoples never fired clay for use as building materials. They had ample supplies of wood for building homes. Although fired at very low temperatures their cooking-pots were remarkably thin (averaging about 5 to 7mm) for three or four thousand years of the Incipient and the beginnings of the Initial phase. The pots' thinness resulted in their being fired right through with no black core. Fired cooking-pots were rather porous but retained water long enough to serve for cooking. Ethnographic evidence from around the world shows that plant juices are widely used to seal the inside surfaces of porous earthenware. Such juices are often applied while the pot is still hot from its firing. The Jomon did not, however, at any time realize the advantages of enclosed kilns to achieve temperatures at which some clays vitrify to form non-porous bodies.

Incipient Jomon pots were not large. They might have been built 'upside down', from top to bottom, by joining small sheets made from balls of clay, kneaded, flattened and shaped by hand. Perhaps to gain height, it appears that, at least towards the rim, coils of clay were added and flattened. From many widely separated sites the effects of firing on the pots are very similar. They are a greyish-buff colour but marked by the unevenness of the flames. Japanese archaeologists and ceramicists and their students have carried out many experiments and have successfully reproduced sherds and vessels very similar to the originals.

To assess and appreciate Jomon pots for what they are, we must visualize that every one was fired in an open bonfire. From present-day evidence in Africa, New Guinea, Borneo and other regions, it would appear that the pots were stacked on flat or slightly depressed ground with firewood piled over them. Goto (1980) surmised that in Japan the clay was kneaded, shaped, dried and fired in the spring, late summer, or autumn, and that there would have been none of these activities during the mid-summer rainy season or the winter. The jars must have been thoroughly dried beforehand to prevent cracking. The fuel was probably brushwood, but reeds or grasses are other possibilities.

It is noteworthy that, during the whole Jomon period, the temperatures at which pots were fired in the open were extremely low when compared with present earthenware firing temperatures in industry, which range in the vicinity of 1,100°C. Many Japanese archaeologists place the Incipient and later Jomon temperature ranges as low as 500°C or 600°C, but Goto (1980) says that temperatures between 700°C and 900°C were needed. Serizawa (personal communication) believes temperatures to have been between 700°C and 800°C from Initial Jomon through to the end of the Yayoi period (*c.* AD 300). In opposition to Goto and Serizawa, Kidder (personal communication) points out that sherds of much Jomon pottery after the Initial phase show change on both inner and outer surfaces, but not the core. This may indicate that fierce heat had not penetrated right through the body. His students over the years have made many Jomon-type vessels experimentally at temperatures as low as about 500°C. (Other archaeologists make Late Jomon copies at about 700°C to 800°C.) Although experiments have shown that it is possible to create temperatures up to 900°C with open fires, Kidder thinks that such temperatures were not reached until the Late phase of Jomon pottery production. Speculation on temperatures is material only if linked with discussion on both the quality of the clay and the firing time. Similar results may sometimes be obtained by firing at high temperatures for a short time or at lower temperatures for a longer time. In all cases the initial temperature had to be low to prevent cracks.

Goto gives a firing time of about fifty minutes and Kidder agrees that this time was probable. Serizawa suggests several hours and some other archaeologists assume the possibility of longer firing times of up to five or six hours. At Akigawa City,

Tokyo, Keally has watched a Japanese archaeologist, Hanjuro Shiono, produce a pot with every appearance of being Jomon by firing it on level ground on its side. Shiono's small fire, that barely covered the pot, was made entirely by burning grass, handfuls of which Shiono (who was overseeing an excavation in progress nearby) added to keep the small flames burning at an even temperature for about five hours. He had found that pots cracked when exposed to great heat at the start of firing, especially when burnished so that the evaporation of their moisture was retarded. Shiono suggested that the firing of early Jomon pots was started in hot ashes, or a slow fire for an hour or so, before the fire was built up to greater intensity. We tend to think of fires being started with kindling wood at the bottom of the pile. However, the initially low heat could possibly have been achieved almost accidentally by building fires with the 'kindling wood', probably dried grass, piled above the heavy firewood, not below it.

Initial Phase (*c.* 7,500–4,500 BC)

During the Initial Jomon phase, inverted construction, if it had been employed earlier, had given way to vessel-building with coils of clay from the base up. Other techniques remained similar to those of the Incipient phase. Initial Jomon pottery, a little thicker and a little larger that the Incipient, was still thin and, of course, unglazed. Late in the phase many vessels were tempered with fibre. Their colour ranged from grey-brown to dark brown and occasionally reddish with fire-blackened patches.

Early Phase (*c.* 4,500–3,000 BC)

By the Early phase firing temperatures seem to have been increased a little, perhaps to around 700°C, but pots were being made larger and their walls thicker (averaging 9mm to 10mm). Apparently the firing cycle was not slowed down to allow the heat to penetrate evenly these thicker walls. Consequently the cross-section of most surviving Early phase sherds reveals that, between well fired outer surfaces, the centre was left a different colour. Early Jomon pots did not retain water as well as Incipient vessels.

Although pot-walls were becoming thicker in Early Jomon, they tended to crack and deteriorate from the bottom up as their flat bases were less heavily constructed than the pointed and curved bases of the wares of the Initial phase. Short-cut vegetable fibres were frequently mixed as temper into the clay, possibly to improve vapour escape during firing (illustration J19). The fibres burned out leaving irregular impressions and rough uneven surfaces. Towards the end of Early Jomon tempering with fibre gave way to the use of grit (illustration J24).

Middle Phase (*c.* 3,000–2,000 BC)

As early as the Incipient Jomon phase and more frequently during Early Jomon much cooking was done indoors. Evidence of fireplaces is found in many pit-dwellings and all cooking fires had moved inside by the end of Middle Jomon when the elimination of the centre-pole had opened up the interior space. It is more difficult to distinguish whether fires were built inside dwellings after the Middle Jomon phase as pit-dwellings gradually gave way to houses built at ground level. It seems reasonably certain, however, that fires inside houses were not at any time used for pottery-making. This appears to have been carried on outside during the whole Jomon period and it is even more certain that enclosed kilns were not constructed for the firing of pottery.

Firing temperatures during Middle Jomon were probably about 700°C. Thick walls were often consistently fired throughout, their cores a different colour from their buff to brown surfaces. In some Kanto region types, Atamadai (Otamadai) and its contemporary Katsuzaka (Katsusaka), mica is present in the grit used for tempering. Some Atamadai bodies were laminated in two layers, the inner being of purer clay. It is difficult to understand how the lamination was achieved as the pots appear to have been coil-made. Perhaps the second layer was added as a kind of coating after the coils of the first layer had been flattened.

Technical advances are noticeable. Some pots of both Atamadai and Katsuzaka types have rather thin walls with hard well smoothed surfaces, evenly fired with signs of tempering carefully obscured, but most Middle Jomon vessels are large and heavily potted. The Kasori E type pottery (also of the Kanto region) came late in the Middle phase and began a tendency towards a thinner wall.

Late Phase (*c.* 2,000–1,000 BC)

Whereas Jomon vessels during the Middle phase had been robust and heavily potted, Late vessels are less elaborate but usually more carefully made. Particularly in the Kanto and Tohoku regions, improvements in fabrication and firing, already apparent in the Kasori E pottery near the end of Middle Jomon, became more significant during the Late Jomon phase. Some clay was more carefully selected and better worked. Many pots were still heavy, but some were much thinner, averaging about 6 to 7mm. Thin walls required more care at all stages of manufacture, including firing. The cross-sections reveal that the clay was fired more uniformly. Finishing of some pots received greater attention and the pots show more refinement. Walls were often meticulously smoothed and burnished for appearance or to reduce porosity, but in the Kanto region burnishing was losing favour towards the end of Late Jomon.

Perhaps there were a few potters who devoted more time to potting than their predecessors and so became specialized. They certainly exhibited skill, but it must not be overlooked that the majority of pots found in all Late Jomon village sites were simple, coarse utilitarian wares.

Before Late Jomon, colour had ranged from a dull, earthy greyish, or yellowish to buff and brown, but at all times was so varied that generalizations can be misleading. In the first part of the Late Jomon phase many vessels were light brown. By the end of the phase dark brown was more usual, and blue-black, intentionally darkened, had appeared.

Final Phase (c. 1,000–300 BC)

Over the millennia the Jomon potters had learned to select more suitable clay, to work it better and to raise the firing temperature a little, perhaps by locating their fires on slopes to promote better air circulation. Although no kiln structure has ever been found for the Jomon period, the uncovering of burned earth in some recent excavations hints at the possibility of some use of primitive 'kilns' in Yayoi and even Jomon times by fires lit in deep depressions with natural 'chimneys'. A further possibility is that large sherds from old and broken pots covered the new pots during the firing, thus conserving the heat from the embers below.

During the Final Jomon phase in Western Japan and Kyushu there was little technical development, but the level of the improvement in Eastern Japan indicates that pottery-making there had become relatively specialized. There, a large number of ritual vessels exhibit great skill together with a refined quality. The Tohoku region of Eastern Japan became the centre of the greatest pottery production and the most advanced technology but, after the mid-point of Final Jomon, some regression took place. In Eastern Japan vessels tended to be smaller than their predecessors and many walls were hard, smooth, impervious to water and remarkably thin, often averaging about 4 to 5mm. Nevertheless, all pottery throughout Japan was still hand-coiled or moulded without the potter's wheel. Pots were many shades of brown, but black had become quite common and this indicates a change of firing technique.

Outside Contacts

Incipient Phase (c. 10,000–c. 7,500 BC)

There is substantial evidence that the Jomon created earthenware cooking-pots about 12,000 years ago (10,000 BC). For the following 2,000 years there is no evidence yet of pottery (except figurines) having been made in any other part of the world with the possible exception of Siberia. A small number of sherds recently reported from Siberia may be about the same age as the Incipient Jomon. However, transmission between the two countries around 10,000 BC is extremely doubtful and there is no evidence to support the possibility. If the Siberian data is reliable, then it is more probable that pottery was created indigenously and independently in both areas.

Initial Phase (*c. 7,500–c. 4,500 BC*)

Soviet Maritime Provinces and Hokkaido   For about 6,000 years, there is no further evidence reported of pottery production in Siberia. Then there is evidence of trade in obsidian, and also of pottery and stone tools from the Memanbetsu site in north-west Hokkaido, which indicates a close link with Siberia around the middle of the Initial phase. The beginnings and early development of pottery in the Soviet Maritime Provinces are still not clear. In the sixth millennium BC some stone tools there and in central and northern Hokkaido were very similar and the natural environments of both regions were much the same. Cold-temperate forests clothe both shores facing the Sea of Japan. Jomon Akatsuki type pottery in Hokkaido preceded the Memanbetsu type by several centuries. The Yubetsu technique of stone microblade manufacture associated with Akatsuki pottery is considerably older than Memanbetsu and Siberian stone blade points. The punctated-design pottery and the blade points (higashi kushiro) similar to Siberian implements found at Memanbetsu in Hokkaido were a short-lived phenomenon with no evidence of continuity. If a link is firmly established, it would point to Siberia having learned to produce pottery from Hokkaido rather than the reverse.

It should not be overlooked that, if the pottery-making technique was transmitted to Siberia from Hokkaido, it could than have moved from there to Sop'ohang and Osanri on the north-east coast of Korea, as the first pottery recorded in Korea is dated around 6,000 BC.

China and Japan   The earliest pottery in China is now well documented with production in and around Peiligang in North China having commenced about 6,500 BC, and there is a disputed dating of about 8,000 BC in South China. However, no Chinese styles that compare with Initial Jomon, nor any evidence of transmission in either direction, have been found.

Early Phase (*c. 4,500–3,000 BC*)

China and Eastern Japan   Similarity has been suggested between cylindrical pottery found in north-east China and the Ento style Jomon pottery produced in northern Tohoku and Hokkaido. This slender evidence could possibly point to transmission between China and Japan but this has not been verified as there are no supporting circumstances. All evidence points to Early Jomon in Japan being a period of considerable expansion following the demonstrated trend of dispersion of pottery technology within Japan from south to north some millennia previously. It is quite reasonable to suggest that this diffusion, aided by sea-going Jomon fishermen, could have continued beyond Hokkaido, or from a part on the north-west coast of Honshu, but without further evidence this is pure conjecture.

There is no indication that the more advanced Chinese pottery techniques, such as the use of kilns, came to Japan at this time, and suggestions of Chinese influence on Jomon pottery before or during Early Jomon have not been substantiated and appear to be based on a few superficial similarities in appearance.

Korea and Kyushu In Kumamoto-ken, Kyushu, during the Early Jomon phase a distinctive Sobata type developed and spread to embrace southern, northern and western Kyushu (illustrations J30, J31). The Sobata vessels had, above roundish bases, decorative patterns of straight geometric triangles and zig-zags incised with stick-made, deep grooves. Some Sobata jars and bowls are very similar in shape and decoration to 'comb-type' pots of about the fifth millennium found in shell-mounds in Korea at Osan-ri and Tongsam-dong. The pottery of both regions, Kyushu and Korea, discloses so much in common that there is little doubt there were links between them. Following these similarities of decoration contact continued between the two countries throughout Middle, Late and Final Jomon. Jomon 'trade wares' are found in certain southern Korean sites along with obsidian from Kyushu sources. Conversely, many excavations in Japan of Jomon sites have failed to reveal sherds of Korean pots earlier than the third millennium BC. Nevertheless, some Korean and Japanese specialists believe that the Sobata style originated in Korea. They point out that the round-based wares of Sobata are unusual in the general sequence of Jomon shapes and must, therefore, have come from outside Japan. This gives no weight to the fact of everyday life that the craftsmen of any country can create new fashions. This particular style could have originated just as easily in Japan as in Korea. The idea of Korean origination also overlooks the temporal framework. Pottery-making had been established in Japan for thousands of years before the Sobata type evolved, and it seems not unlikely that the Sobata style influenced Korean comb-type pottery, rather than the reverse.[7]

Okinawa and Kyushu The oldest remains of Jomon type pottery found in the Okinawa islands are found in the upper stratum of Akayama in volcanic ash dated to 4,250–4,070 ± 145 BC near the beginning of Early Jomon. (The Noguni and Toguchi Agaribaru sites.) This appears to rule out any possibility of the first pottery made in Japan, about five or six millennia before, having come from Okinawa. In fact, the evidence from the Okinawa islands strongly suggests an Early Jomon migration of people by boat from Kyushu which is about 500 kilometres to the north. While there is, so far, no evidence of pottery transmission into Japan during Early Jomon, there could have been dissemination from Japan.

Middle Phase (*c.* 3,000–2,000 BC)

During the Middle Jomon phase the Jomon had become proficient fishermen with navigable seacraft, and contact with the Asian continent was to be expected. However, there appears to be no firm evidence of significant out-side contact on pottery of this phase.

Late Phase (*c.* 2,000–1,000 BC)

Kyushu and Korea Kyushu reflected a minor continental influence during Late Jomon. In north-west Kyushu Late Jomon and contemporary south-east Korean (Tongsam-dong) pots still had similarities that indicate contact between the countries. The main direction of influence is still uncertain.

Japan and the Amur Valley (Siberia) Some vessels found in the Amur Valley on the Asian continent between Manchuria and Siberia imply a temporary development parallel with the Kasori B style which was diffused through much of Japan during Late Jomon. It was unlikely that potters from the Amur Valley had to come to Japan. The long development of the Kasori E and B types within Japan is well evidenced, as is their original provenance in Eastern Japan. Of course, other Amur Valley pottery with ring-feet and pedestals, some perforated, shows clear evidence of Asian mainland tradition.

Final Phase (*c.* 1,000–300 BC)

Japan and the Asian continent Contact with the Asian mainland could have been aided by the Black Current from the equator, part of which flows along the coast of China and Korea. It carried debris to the Sea of Japan as far north as the Tohoku region. The possibility fits well with Wilhelm Solheim's theory of 'boat people' plying trade along the east coast of China. They could have reached Kyushu and even further north looking for new products and markets while leaving behind rice and perhaps some small colonies. However, there is no hard evidence of these boat people having reached Japan. If they had it would not have been before the end of Late Jomon as the rice they might have brought has not been found earlier.

During the Final Jomon phase interchange between Kyushu and the Asian continent was slowly growing. Cist-graves, jar burials, spindle-whorls for fabric weaving, stone reaping-knives, and rice appeared. Pottery in Kyushu tended to have plainer surfaces. The new influence on pottery came with rice cultivation, originally from east-coast China by the boat people, or by way of the south Korean peninsula. Evidence of continental influence on Western Japanese culture presaged the over-whelming changes seen in the following Yayoi period, but this influence was at first confined almost solely to Kyushu. Korean and Kyushu pottery techniques, shapes and designs slowly converged during the last millennium BC until some of the pottery of the next Japanese (Early Yayoi) period was nearly the same as that of south Korea.

Also in the Final Jomon phase the Western Japan Kurotsuchi type, coarse functional pots with narrow bases and heavily scraped bodies, usually had plain surfaces except for notched ridges encircling rims and shoulders. It is similar in some way to contemporary Korean and Chinese pottery, and to the following Yayoi period pottery. It indicates a possible link with the pottery of China's Shandong Peninsula.

It has been conjectured that some Obora designs hint at Chinese decoration, perhaps brought to Japan by the boatmen. The 'flowing water' pattern, ryusuimon (illustrations J133, J134) is long established on Chinese pottery. Kidder has also suggested that some Obora designs might have been stylized Chinese dragons, and could have come from the decoration of Chinese bronze mirrors. During the Yayoi period which followed the Jomon, mirrors were given to Japanese leaders by Chinese courts of the Han period. Perhaps some had reached Eastern Japan during the Final Jomon phase but, although Chinese-like ritual weapons were transmitted, no mirrors have yet been found. Other such links common from the Late phase could have been the pedestalled bowls, especially those with perforated stems.

Until the Yayoi period the continental influence, so strong in Kyushu, had little if any impact on the neighbouring main island of Honshu. Jomon style pots continued to be made undisturbed in the rest of Japan, particularly in the north-east and Hokkaido, for many centuries after the end of the Jomon period in Western Japan.

Types, Styles and Sites

Types

In classifying types it must be taken into account that every Jomon pot was hand made by individuals who, until the Late and Final phases, were hardly likely to have been full-time specialists. Pots were made when pots were needed. On present-day ethnographic evidence the craft would have been learned from within the family. Most likely, a mother taught her daughter. In meeting the needs of their families and the immediate community, potters shared in the local and conservative traditions of shape and decoration. However, by the evidence of the pots excavated from hundreds of sites it appears that whereas tradition ensured continuity of motifs and their preservation, it also left room for expressions of individuality as well as local preferences. Classification of types is complex and far from standardized.

Jomon pottery has been loosely segmented into more than two hundred types and sub-types. Variations of types and nomenclature and classifications have followed the whims of archaeologists who in the past have shown a tendency to give a new type name to pottery they have excavated from their own sites, especially if the sites have yielded many vessels. In the text and end notes of this book, type names mainly follow what one archaeologist (Kidder, 1968:286) has chosen as the main types in each region in each phase, but alternative names employed by other archaeologist are scattered in the text. The end notes list about thirty types for each phase, but even this large number is far from all embracing and does not cover the many alternative choices of other archaeologists. There is no generally accepted overall classification.

To draw a balanced picture, a researcher must study representative collections of each type of pottery and group the types into broad units to reduce the mass of type names while taking account of shapes, decoration, established datings and regional distribution. This has rarely been attempted since Yamanouchi's pioneering work of the 1930s when only a fraction of today's material had been excavated. However, recently Kobayashi (1983) has reduced the great number of type and site names in common usage to sixty-six style names. This still large number of styles is listed in an end note.[8] Kobayashi's classification is a great step forward, but it may take some time before this style names replace those currently used. Kidder's types and Kobayashi's styles are steps towards a chronological and regional overview, but they many yet be modified in the search for a more balanced classification.

The types named in the text and in end note synopses may be added to, or reduced, by serious students. Amended enumerations will vary with the authorities consulted. There is no unanimity. Whichever types are chosen, the sheer number reveals the volume and intensity of the investigations being carried out by Japanese archaeologists.

The Jomon people created pots as fire-proof containers for cooking food. This was the sole function of all Incipient phase vessels and, during all the following phases, was overwhelmingly their most common usage. Archaeologists employ the Japanese word 'fukabachi' to describe the shape of the Incipient phase vessels and their descendants. This word is sometimes translated into English as 'deep bowl'. This creates an inaccurate mental picture of their shape. The height of a fukabachi exceeds the diameter of its wide mouth. The fukabachi of the earliest years could be translated as 'cooking-pots', which all were, but vessels of the same shape came to be used also for storage and carrying. At this stage 'jar' becomes a more appropriate word and replaces fukabachi in this book.

Incipient Phase (*c.* 10,000–7,500 BC)

Many of the Incipient Jomon sherds that have been recovered are little larger than the size of postage stamps. Vessels are difficult to restore. Edges and surfaces crumble. Only a few of the oldest pots have been reconstructed. Base sherds are rare as the bottoms of many vessels have virtually disintegrated. Vessels from Sempukuji (colour plate C1), Kamino (colour plate C2), Muroya (illustrations J2–J5) and Omotedate (illustration J1h) have all been reconstructed from sherds. The sizes of the very first pots can only be calculated from the curvature of the small sherds which have so far been found, but most experts estimate diameters of about 15cm to 22cm with similar heights.

The naming of types is as indefinite in the Incipient Jomon phase as in the following phases. Over this first, long phase some archaeologists name Ichinosawa, Hashidate, Yanagimata and Ishigoya types in addition to the standard decoration-style and site names. Here we will comment on only a few of the oldest sites: Fukui cave and Sempukuji rock-shelters in Nagasaki-ken; Kamikuroiwa rock-shelter in Ehime-ken; Kosegasawa and Muroya caves in Niigata-ken; and Kamino site, which is neither a rock-shelter nor a cave, in Kanagawa-ken near Tokyo.

Fukui was the first of the most ancient sites to be explored and radiocarbon dated. This sandstone cave overlooking the Fukui river in Nagasaki-ken, eastern Kyushu, revealed the continuity between pre-ceramic and ceramic stages of Japan's prehistoric culture. The Fukui site has been excavated down to 15 levels. The base level held a large flake assemblage to which radiocarbon tests have given an age of about 30,000 BC (Serizawa, 1976). Level 4, without pottery, had obsidian microblades and wedge-shaped microcores together with scrapers of andesite.

Incipient Jomon sherds in its third level were radiocarbon dated to about $10,700 \pm 500$ BC (Gak, 950), the earliest pottery known when the Fukui site was excavated. Microblades and microcores similar to Level 4 were also present. These Level 3 pottery sherds with relatively broad bands of modelled relief were found together with others of fine-line relief and 'nail-marking'. The overlying Level 2 had more fine-line relief and nail-marking but without microliths. Nail-marked sherds dominated in the upper part of this level, $10,400 \pm 240$ BC (Gak, 949).

Sempukuji rock-shelters set into a sandstone cliff in Sasebo-shi, Nagasaki-ken, Kyushu, open onto a slope facing south, 89 metres above sea level. The shelters contain strata up to 2 metres thick. These strata have yielded materials from the late Upper Palaeolithic (knife-shaped tools) to the early historic Heian period. The most outstanding remains belong to the microlithic culture of the terminal Palaeolithic and the beginning of the Incipient Jomon pottery-bearing culture, the peak of habitation intensity at the site.

Sempukuji disclosed a stratum bearing nail-marked and linear relief sherds similar to Fukui Level 3. In contrast, the stratum *below* at Sempukuji has yielded sherds of a completely new type which featured an appliqué of bean-shaped lumps (colour plate C1). Within this layer microblades and their cores were also found in association with the unique sherds. The lumps (or lozenges) were named 'bean-relief' or, in Japanese, toryumon. They are about 1cm long and 1–1 + 1/2cm wide.

Comparison between the stratigraphic sequences of Fukui and Sempukuji reveals a similar pattern of primitive pottery emerging from a culture using microblades. In both cases the culture then ceased to use microblades but continued with pottery. Although carbon datings appear to make Fukui sherds older than Sempukuji's, the Sempukuji sequence reveals a distinctive, and so far unique, stratum where toryumon pottery precedes the linear relief and nail-marked pottery in both sites. Dating of the Semukuji site has been done through direct and indirect cross-checking of radiocarbon, thermoluminescence and obsidian fission-track age measurements. The different dating systems are independent of each other and each produces its own figures. From these tests dates of *c.* 10,500–8,500 BC have been given for the toryumon stratum. There can be no doubt about the extreme age of the toryumon pottery style, or that pottery making had its beginning in the microlithic stage.

Kamikuroiwa rock-shelter, at Mikawa-machi, Kamiukena-shi, Ehime-ken on Shikoku (now a separate island but a part of Honshu until about 6,000/7,000 BC) was excavated after Fukui and before Sempukuji. It is in limestone country and its dating perhaps less certain than other sites. Pottery sherds radiocarbon dated at 10,155 ± 600 BC were reported and are said to be similar to the oldest at Fukui and the sherds found in the level above the lowest at Sempukuji. Embellished with parallel bands of fine linear relief, the recovered sherds indicate that the vessels were deep, round-based pots. This single date is not strong evidence, but it suggests that the Kyushu pottery was a little older.

Kosegasawa is a cave site in central Honshu. Situated on the middle slopes of Mount Kosegasawa it overlooks the Muroya river about 60 kilometres south of Niigata city. About 1,000 pottery sherds have been recovered there. At its lowest level, a few linear relief sherds are analogous to those of Fukui, Sempukuji and Kamikuroiwa. Here again, a slightly younger age suggests an eastward diffusion of the technology. Pottery of the level above was stick-impressed and nail-marked. At about 7,500 BC the cave entrance was blocked by a land-fall.

Muroya cave, in Niigata-ken, not very far from Kosegasawa, is another of the early, but not earliest, Incipient Jomon sites. Recovered Incipient phase vessels (illustrations J2–J5), some cord indented, are more complete than those from the most ancient sites. They are earlier than 7,500 BC. The cave remained in occupation for a very long time and pottery of later phases has been recovered from upper levels (Nakamura and Ogata, 1964).

Kamino, part of the Tsukimono/Kamino group of sites in Kanagawa-ken, near Tokyo, is one of several sites along the banks of the old Sakai river and its tributary the Meguro river (other nearby locations are Megurogawa-Togan, Kamiwada-Shirayama and Fukami-Suwayama). In Yokohama, only about 10 kilometres from Kamino, Hanamiyama and Tsukidematsu sites have also been explored.[9] These sites were in open country, not caves or rock-shelters. All have yielded very old, linear relief sherds. The oldest, from the Kamino site, are dated by thermoluminescence to about 11,900–10,100 BC.

Kamino sherds from the lowest ceramic level have not been restored but others, dated by thermoluminescence to about 10,800 BC, have been used in reassembling a pot (about 22cm high with mouth diameter about 23cm). It is notable for applied relief formed from thin strips of clay pressed on to make a regular pattern of diamond shapes encircling the body of the pot below deep horizontal grooves below the rim, and lower grooving (colour plate C2). The Kamino decoration appears to be more sophisticated and therefore later than Semukuji's more primitive bean-shaped lumps, but a clear relationship between radiocarbon and thermoluminescence dating is not yet determined and comparisons are not straightforward as the earliest Kamino sherds are fragmentary. Some Japanese archaeologists believe Kamino sherds to be the oldest so far discovered (Fukuda, personal communication, 1987).

Initial Phase (*c. 7,500–4,500 BC*)

For Initial Jomon, as many as forty-three named types are listed in an end note,[10] for a phase which covers three thousand years. Some of these types are illustrated: Natsushima (illustration J6), Hanawadai (J7), Inaridai (J8), Tado (J9),Unoki (J10), Kayama (J11), and Sumiyoshicho (J12). One type, Natsushima, here classified as Initial, but treated as Incipient by many archaeologists, deserves a brief description of its excavation.

Natsushima shell-mound, which has given its name to the type, is located on a small island (now joined to the mainland) in Tokyo Bay at Yokosuka just south of Yokohama. It was excavated shortly after the Second World War and was the scene for the very first introduction of scientific dating for Japanese archaeology.

Radiocarbon determination of the age of materials recovered with the pottery at Natsushima provided a dramatic result. An age of around 7,300 BC was indicated and this contradicted the established opinion that no Jomon pottery was earlier than about 2,500 BC. At the time this result was widely rejected by the archaeological establishment, but when even earlier dates came to be indicated for other sites there was a gradual accommodation to the new evidence. Even so, Sugao Yamanouchi, the brilliant pioneer of Jomon typology, was not alone in never being able to accept the validity of radiocarbon testing and the resulting long chronology. Today the Natsushima results are accepted by the majority, as are the results for many sites that are much older. They fit well into today's overall Jomon chronology (end notes 11–15).

Seven levels were traced throughout the Natsushima mound. The lower six levels are Initial phase and the upper (Level 7) is Early phase. The second from bottom cultural layer is dated 7,290 ± 500 BC. Over 10,000 sherds were excavated altogether. The nine vessels completely restorable were all conical with pointed or rounded bottoms (illustration J6). On pottery of the lowest level, cord-marking applied to the whole surface was present on more than ninety per cent of all outer surfaces. At Level 3 cord-marking becomes rare and in Layers 4 to 6 the predominant decorations are grooving, shell-impressing and shell scraping (kaigaramon).[11]

The Inaridai type (J8), similar to and produced about the same time as the Natsushima type, is named from Inari-cho, Iidabashi-ku, Tokyo, about 30 kilometres east of Natsushima. Grooved and shell-marked styles were identified first at Tado (J9), Kayama (J11) and other sites which have also given their names to types.

To the south-west, Kyushu, thought by some to be the home of Incipient Jomon pottery, continued in production during the Initial phase. Two new types have been recorded, Iwashita and Todoroki Lower. Further excavations will undoubtedly reveal more pottery but the styles do not yet appear to have changed to any great extent.

To the extreme north, the oldest pots so far identified in Hokkaido have been excavated from Akatsuki, with one piece tentatively dated about 6,500 BC. Other very early types in Hokkaido were Monomidai, between 6,200 and 6,000 BC; Sumiyoshicho (illustration J12) between 5,900 and 5,500 BC; Kojohama, about 5,700 BC; and Higashi Kushiro, about 5,100 BC. Another early Hokkaido type, Memanbetsu, has already been mentioned because of its close link with Siberian pottery. Surface upheavals and subsidences through millennia of heavy frosts make dating at some sites uncertain and excavations have not been as numerous or intense in Hokkaido as on the other main islands of Japan. However, at present there is no evidence that they will match in age the oldest Incipient Jomon vessels scattered widely over Kyushu, Shikoku and Honshu.

Early Phase (*c.* 4,500–3,000 BC)

The number of types now named proliferated. For the roughly fifteen hundred years of the Early Jomon phase, forty-two types may be listed.[12] Types illustrated include Sekiyama (illustrations J13/J15); Nuname (J16); Ento Lower (C5, J17); Hanazumi Lower (J18, J19); Okitsu (J20); Moroiso (C6, J21/J27); Fukura (J28); Kitashirakawa (J29); and Sobata (J30, J31).

In all phases type distinctions are based on variations in decoration and shapes but most of the type names listed are from sites. Ento (which translates as cylindrical) is an exception and is given to pots from a wide area. The Ento name was coined by an eminent early anthropologist (Kotundo Hasebe) and has been retained for a wide range of vessels of the northern Tohoku region and also in south-western Hokkaido. Later archaeologists have sub-divided the type into Ento Lower (Early Jomon phase) with seven chronological groups, and Ento Upper (Middle Jomon phase) with five. (Neighbouring the Ento area to its south, the rather similar Daigi type from a shell-mound in Shichigama-machi, Shiogama-shi in the southern

Tohoku region has also been divided into twelve stages covering the Early and Middle Jomon phases.)

Moroiso type (C6, J21–J27) is a name originally given to finds from early excavations of a shell-mound in the Miura Peninsula, Kanagawa-ken, in the Kanto region. It is now divided into Moroiso A, B and C. Some Moroiso vessels were fibre-tempered, but the type is noted for its cord-marking, stick-grooving, nail-marking and superimposed clay strips and button-like clay lumps. Moroiso is still used as a generic name for the most abundant style of the latter half of Early Jomon in the Kanto, Chubu and Kansai regions.

The Kitashirakawa type (J29) found in the Torihama shell-mound located on low-lying, damp ground on the Japan Sea coast of Fukui-ken, is also well distributed through the Kansai region. It was, except for its local clay, very similar to the Moroiso type.

Middle Phase (*c.* 3,000–2,000 BC)

About twenty Middle Jomon types have been separately named.[13] Of these, the following are illustrated: Shimpo (J31a, J31b); Atamadai (J32/J33); Katsuzaka (C9, J34/J47); Nashikubo (J48); Tonai (J49/J51); Umataka (C7, J52/J55); Ento Upper (J56, J57); Daigi (J58, J59); Idojiri (J60, J61); Monzen (J62); Sori (J63); and Kasori E (C8, J64/J72).

Many of these styles proliferated within the densely populated Kanto and Chubu regions of Central Japan. During the Middle phase certain pairs (or sets) of these styles appear to have coexisted with a region, but without coinciding. What this means is that whereas their distribution clearly over-laps, the two styles are not found together on the same site. The cultural significance of this close-grained separation is interesting but, once again, is not yet understood.

Examples of such coexisting types are:

1. Goryogadai, Shimono (Kanto): Nashikubo, Aramichi (Chubu).
2. Katsuzaka 1, 2, Atamadai 1, 2 (Kanto): Tonai, Idojiri (Chubu).
3. Katsuzaka 3, Atamadai 3 (Kanto): Chojagahara, Umataka (Chubu).
4. Kasori E 1A, 1B, 2, 3, 4 (Kanto): Sori (Chubu).

(Keally: personal communication)

Around the middle of the Middle Jomon phase, Atamadai (J32, J33) and Katsuzaka (C9 J34/J47) types of the Kanto evolved into succeeding types, predominantly the Kasori E (C8, J64/J72) type (first excavated from the Kasori shell-mounds of Chiba City on the east coast of Tokyo Bay). In Yamanashi-ken, Chubu region, the Katsuzaka-related Idojiri type evolved into Sori (J63) which is very similar to Kasori E. All over the Kanto and neighbouring provinces transitions were very gradual.

In northern Tohoku, as stated earlier, the Ento Upper type (J56, J57) with five chronological stages appropriately numbered links with four more stages in south-western Hokkaido that carry the same type name. The Ento type is quite distinct from the Katsuzaka/Kasori E–Idojiri/Sori group of related styles further south. In southern Tohoku (north of the Kanto and Chubu regions) the Daigi (J58, J59) type has five temporal divisions. Some late Daigi types resemble neighbouring Kasori E.

Western Japan was influenced by the gradual evolution in central and northern Honshu but, as far as is known at present, during the whole of the Middle Jomon phase its relatively scarce pottery appears to have changed little.

Late Phase (*c.* 2,000–1,000 BC)

During the Late Jomon phase distinctions in pottery between northern and central Honshu diminished, but in the Tohoku region to the north technology and decoration appear to have advanced more than in the Kanto. At least thirty main types have classed as Late Jomon.[14] Those illustrated are Shomyoji (J73); Horinouchi (C10, J74/J80); Tokoshinai (J81/J83, J98): Kasori B (C11, J84/J97); Oyu (J99, J100); Angyo (J101/J106); Shinchi (J107, J108).

The Kanto region Shomyoji type (J73) which straddled the end of Middle Jomon and the early part of Late Jomon, comes from the Shomyoji group of small shell-mounds in what is now Yokohama city. Shomyoji pots had wide mouths and expanding rims, slightly bulging shoulders on bodies which tapered to smaller, occasionally very small, flat bases. Some Shomyoji pots had the peaked rims of Middle Jomon style. Others had a squaring of the rims not uncommon in the Late Jomon phase.

The Horinouchi type (C10, J74/J80) named after the Horinouchi shell-mound near Chiba city east of Tokyo, evolved from the Shomyoji type. Some vessels (J74) could be Shomyoji or Horinouchi 1. The Horinouchi type, a classic ware of the first half of Late Jomon, dominated the Kanto region before Kasori B. Similar types are found north through the Tohoku region and south-west to the Shikoku and West Honshu regions around the Inland Sea.

Kasori B (C11, J84/J97) is named from pots from a different part and higher levels of the shell-mound in Chiba-ken in the Kanto region which preserved such a wealth of Middle Jomon, Kasori E pottery. In the Kanto region, in the second half of Late Jomon, a natural development had run through Kasori B into the earliest Angyo types (J101/J106). Angyo 1 was only a little different from Kasori B in its use of low horizontal ridges interspersed with small hemispherical lumps. Angyo 2 was the most impressive of the Angyo stages.

The early Late Jomon Tokoshinai type (J81/J83, J98) of the north Tohoku region, and the Shinchi type (J107, J108) from Fukushima-ken in southern Tohoku, had much in common with the Horinouchi type. The Tokoshinai

Jomon Pottery

type was also related to the large Kasori B family. In northern Tohoku, linked with the Horinouchi cultural stage, there was also a minor, linear incised, Oyu type (J99, J100) which is found around the great stone circles of Akita-ken.

In the first half of Late Jomon, in Western Japan from the Kansai region as far south as Shikoku, equivalents of the Horinouchi type of the Kanto were made. Adopted slightly later in western Shikoku, some minor types must also be connected with Kasori B of the Kanto.

Towards the end of Late Jomon the Mimanda type from the Kumamoto area in southern Kyushu, shell-scraped and shell-marked, was made of dark, hard clay in a range of shapes which in addition to the standard cooking-pots included dishes, bowls and high, wide-necked pouring pots. Found together with them were a number of figurines which were not widely produced in other parts of Kyushu.

The Goryo type of Miyazaki-ken in south-east Kyushu, an off-shoot of the Mimanda type, had the last of the fine surface finishes in the south. Goryo shapes were mainly bowls and strongly shouldered jars with collared rims and often raised feet. Walls were thin and highly polished.

Final Phase (c. 1,000–300 BC)

Overall there were at least thirty types during Final Jomon,[15] but one type group, Obora, overshadowed all others. Previously known as Kamegaoka, that name derives from a large peat-bog along the banks of the Iwaka River in Kizukuri-machi, near Kamegaoka, about 40 kilometres west from Aomori city, North Tohoku region. The style is associated with a remarkable range of Final Jomon pottery found in great quantity over an extensive area. For about a hundred years before archaeologists had a chance to examine them carefully, Kamegaoka sites were plundered. Quantities of Kamegaoka vessels are held by private collectors and museums throughout Japan and overseas.

Until recently Kamegaoka was generally used as an inclusive name for the most outstanding and widely produced pottery style of Final Jomon. Now, after intensive examination of well stratified shell-mounds in Ofunato Bay, Iwate-ken, adjacent to Aomori-ken, the Kamegaoka style name has officially given way to the name Obora type, which is defined in a temporal sequence. Obora vessels are illustrated (C12, C13, J109/J134) and also Kashiwara (J135/J137).

The wide-ranging, supra-regional Obora type was produced all over Eastern Japan and beyond. Spreading from its centre, the Tohoku region, the type soon appears in Hokkaido and the east, central and west coasts of northern Honshu. It influenced the Kanto region (where Final Jomon remains are rather rare) and much of Western Japan. The diversity of the Obora type is shown in the illustrations (J109/J134).

46

Decorative Techniques

Cord-marking

For almost the whole Jomon period and over most the country, Jomon potters adorned their vessels with surface markings or appliqué. Cord-marking was the most favoured technique, particularly in Eastern Japan, but rouletting with carved sticks, applied and linear relief, 'stab and drag' grooving, shell-marking and scraping also played significant roles. Cord, bamboo and occasionally shells served as tools for impressing the plastic clay.

That the whole period has been given the generic name Jomon, or cord-marked, is appropriate as variations of this method of decorating are to be found on so many pots from around 7,500 BC (the Incipient/Initial transition) and thereafter down the ages to the end of the Jomon period (*c.* 300 BC). Even in the following Yayoi period and later, cord-marking is clearly shown on many vessels in Eastern Japan. However, not all Jomon pottery was cord-marked and this decoration was more common east and north of the Japanese Alps than in Western Japan. In Kyushu it was rare throughout the whole of the Jomon period.

One peculiarity distinguishes Jomon vessels. In many countries, and particularly in Asia, early potters smoothed and hardened their coil-formed products by beating the walls on the outside with some kind of cord-covered or grooved 'paddle', while they held an 'anvil' (a smooth stone or other hard object) inside. There is no evidence that the Jomon used beaters. Instead, they smoothed down the surfaces with their fingers, or they might sometimes have used smooth stone or wood as pressure devices. The cord-marking on Jomon pots was pressed or rolled on, not from beaters.

The most ancient cord impressions were made by finger-pressure of thick cords on the damp clay surfaces as seen on the rims of pots from the Muroya cave in Niigata-ken (J2/J5). This primitive cord-indenting typified the last stage of decoration of the Incipient phase.

In the 1930s Sugao Yamanouchi, as an integral part of his approach to dividing the long Jomon period in space and time, studied the cord-marking on every vessel he had to hand. Long before the term 'experimental archaeology' was even invented, Yamanouchi became the first researcher to both analyse and reconstruct the wide variety of cord-marking techniques. Previous pioneers, such as N.G. Munro (1908), had believed the impressed patterns to result from the application of textiles. In the culmination of Yamanouchi's work (*Primitive Arts of Japan*, 1964), Yamanouchi illustrated fourteen basic cords.

The Jomon methods of cord-marking started from taking two strands of cord (probably a single strand doubled and parallel) and forming them into a single strand. Two basics of all cords are the angle and direction of the twists, either from left or right to left. The number of designs achievable by cord-marking is almost limitless, created by various twists and by the use of additional strands.

Some forty years after Yamanouchi's achievement, William M. Hurley has illustrated 271 different patterns and described how each can be created. He points out that these are but a sample of the possibilities. Hurley (1979: 15, 16) writes:

> A cord is the end product of combining two or more strands. The simplest form has two strands of the same composition, diameter and twist. Elaborations can be generated by increasing the number of strands, varying the directions of the twists, employing elements of unequal diameters, altering the process of construction, including knots or loops and introducing other kinds of modification. A two stranded cord may be used alone or as a core for a series of elaborations created by adding one or more supplementary cords after the core has been completed. The supplemental cord or cords have a twist opposite to the components, or final twist, of the core cord . . . Two groups of untwisted strands (or one doubled) are held, attached to or wrapped around a secure object, and each group is twisted in a clockwise (or, alternatively, anticlockwise) direction while being passed hand to hand in the opposite directions.

Cords may be impressed onto the clay before firing as a 'single' mark, or they may be rolled with the palm of the hand onto a vessel's surface. The cord may also be wrapped around whole sticks, or split sticks, or bundles of sticks, or they may be wrapped around a cord core. The sticks were 6cm or shorter with only part of their lengths wrapped. A feature of cord-wrapped stick-marking is that the stick can be wrapped leaving empty space between the cords to make spectacular impressions on the spot. The popular Yoriitomon style of the Initial Jomon phase exemplifies cord-wrapped stick-marking.

After the black and white illustrations of vessels, reproductions of cord-marking from Sahara (1981) are reproduced.

Linear Relief

An outstanding feature of Jomon vessels is that, with only a short break around 8,000 BC, the surfaces of almost all, even the very earliest, were decorated. At the level above Sempukuji's oval lumps came pottery with linear relief, ryusenmon, raised ridges often encircling the vessel near the rim. In the oldest stage ropes of clay were applied to form ridges. Later a fine linear relief was achieved from thinner strips smoothed into the pot surface with fingers and thumbs, or a wide applicating tool probably of bamboo. Kidder (1979) has written:

> Linear relief is so far documented for 32 ancient sites from Nagasaki-ken to Yamagata-ken, a distance of over 1,000 kilometres as the crow flies. Of these 11 are cave sites and 6 rock-shelters. Only in the central area of Japan are the sites open . . . Linear relief has been minutely subdivided into: standard (or

coarse), fine and finest (or thread relief). The coarse consists of applied strips of clay, often indented, sometimes in several horizontal rows near the top of the vessel. The strips may have been originally applied to reinforce junctures before their later acceptance as decoration in the finer relief. They may also have made the pots easier to handle and could have helped to even wall thicknesses.

Other possible practical reasons for linear relief could have been to reduce cracking, or to give strength to the pot-walls. However, this form of decoration must surely also have been intended to give visual satisfaction.

Nail-marking

In stratigraphic sequence above linear relief adornment at Fukui and Sempukuji came 'nail-marking' (tsumegatamon). This was a series of indentations which at first could have been made by finger or thumbnails, but more likely was made by split bamboo impressed into the clay before firing. The bamboo used as a Jomon potter's tool was probably one of the sasa grasses, or other species of small bamboo, split in half lengthwise and the end pressed into the surface of the pot. Nail-marking is found mostly in western Honshu. In Eastern Japan, the Kanto and Chubu regions, a variant style of nail-marking is closer to 'stab and drag' grooving.

Grooving

Grooving is easily achieved by dragging the sharpened tip of a simple tool (such as a stick) across the surface of the unfired pot. Also, by pulling the concave inside of a split bamboo along the surface, grooves in parallel lines were drawn. Triangles were also impressed, probably with sharpened ends of the same bamboo sticks.

An extension of grooving is 'stab and drag', sometimes referred to as 'jab and drag' (chinsemon in Japanese). All this means is that the grooving is punctuated by moments of extra downward pressure.

Rouletting and Shell-marking

An alternative technique, rouletting (oshigatamon) – rolling short, carved sticks across the vessels' surfaces – gave an impressed pattern less densely textured than cord-marking. It showed up in the Kanto region in the late half of the Initial phase (J10) when vessels were rather plain or only lightly cord-marked. Around 6,000 BC rouletting was common all over Western Japan and dominant in Kyushu. Rouletting was rare north of the Kanto region.

In the Kanto region the use of shells for scraping, grooving and indenting is found about 6,000 BC as a main decorative technique. Its adoption followed in the Tohoku region and then Hokkaido (J12) by about 5,500 BC. It was also practised in Kyushu.

Mat-marking

The marks of leaves and mats pressed into the bases of pots before firing have been found in Initial Jomon wares, and from the Early (Torihama shell-mound), Middle (Mitsuzawa shell-mound) and Late (Omori shell-mound) phases. The patterns show that basketry was quite advanced in Japan by the fifth millennium BC. (The weaving of fibres had been evident thousands of years earlier in the use of cord.) The mat-marks resulted from quite strong pressure. They could have been a subtle form of decoration, but it has been suggested that they could indicate the use of mats, or large leaves, as a primitive way of revolving jars before the introduction of any form of the turntable. It would have been easier for a potter to make a vessel by rotating it than by lifting or moving around it. Most bases are not mat-marked. Nevertheless, instead of using mats, the Jomon potters could have placed their vessels on flat stones or other smooth objects which could have been rotated.

Lacquered Pottery

Well preserved, solidly coated, Moroiso-type lacquered pottery from the Ondashi site (C6), Takahara-machi, Yamagata-ken, is dated about 4,500 BC. The lacquer found on Early Jomon pottery is thought to be a ferrous oxide compound mixed with the sap of the Japanese sumac tree (*Rhus verniciflua*). Kimio Suzuki suggests that a complex technique was needed for the lacquering of pottery, and its production shows that the Jomon people had an extensive knowledge of their plant world. He feels that to have reached the stage of making and applying lacquer they had been experimenting with plants much earlier.

Moroiso-type Early Jomon sherds found at the Kamo site (preserved under water along with wooden paddles and the remains of a canoe) had also been coated with a brownish-red lacquer, conceivably to reduce the porosity of storage vessels. This finish is also on Kitashirakawa-type pottery found at the Torihama shell-mound and along the Japan Sea coast of south-western Japan. Such lacquered vessels are also excavated from sites in the following phases. Lacquer is found on many Obora wares of the Final phase. The lacquer was still made from the same species of wild tree that had been used during earlier times.

Unlike the heavy lacquer on the earlier Ondashi site pottery, most lacquering of Jomon earthenware was very lightly applied and unsuitable for surfaces exposed to heat. Often, it has not withstood the ravages of time and is frequently washed off when excavated vessels are being cleaned. The lacquer can then be seen only in the pores of the cleaned surface when examined under a magnifying glass.

What is thought to be the oldest lacquered ware so far discovered in China, from Kaboto near the mouth of the Changjiang, is close in age but may be a little later than the Ondashi ware (Kobayashi, personal communication). The indigenous Jomon development could be the world's earliest application of lacquer to pottery.

Phases: Decoration and Shapes

Incipient Phase (*c.* 10,000–7,500 BC)

Incipient phase pottery appears to have had two basic shapes. Some of the earliest pots with rounded bases could have been inspired by the skin bags and woven baskets which were in common use from earliest times. Others have flat, square bases which Kobayashi believes were modelled from wooden boxes which may also have been in wide use. At Muroya, not the most ancient of the Incipient phase sites, flat bases have been found at the lowest level before rounded ones. The Nakamichi site in Shizuoka-ken has also yielded Incipient pots with flat square bases. However, most Incipient pots had pointed bases (J1h).

Initial Phase (*c.* 7,500–4,500 BC)

Decoration was modest during the first half of Initial Jomon. The cord-marking by finger pressure gave way to rolling. The Yoriitomon group of styles include two kinds of rolled cord-marking. One method, cord-wrapped stick-marking, was to wrap cord of one or more strands around short (6cm or shorter) sticks held between finger and thumb and rolled across the surfaces in long sweeps. The other technique was simply to roll short cords across the vessel's surface in short strokes, pressing down with fingers or the flat hand. Various cord-markings spread extensively from the Kanto region as the predominant decoration of Yoriitomon style pottery during the first half of the Initial Jomon phase.

After its popularity at the beginning of the Initial Jomon phase (C3), cord-marking seems to have dropped out of production countrywide, except in Hokkaido, during the middle and much of the later half of the phase. Shell-marking was popular in the late half of Initial Jomon. Then, near the end of the phase, cord-marking returned in northern Tohoku along with deeply grooved and excised marking.

The Initial Jomon cooking and storage jars were still small, mostly between 20 to 30cm high, wide-mouthed and straight-sided. Rims were sometimes thickened and usually level (J6/J10) but, occasionally, some undulated (J11, J12). Most bases were pointed or bullet-shaped. Very few were flat. Pointed bases, particularly in the Tohoku and Kanto regions, are associated with cord-marking and, in Kyushu, with carved stick rouletting. Some jars had nipple-shaped bases (J10) which had first been made in the Incipient phase (around Omodate, Aomori-ken). These were briefly common in the Kanto/Chubu regions in the middle of the Initial Jomon phase just after the Yoriitomon pots disappeared and before a climax of shell-marking (J12). It is not difficult to visualize the advantages of pointed bases for insertion in soft ground when cooking was outdoors, or flat bases for the more usual flat surfaces, but nipple-pointed bases would seem to have little advantage in any circumstances.

Base sherds throughout Japan are hard to find, but some Initial phase bases have been recovered intact while the sides above them have disintegrated. It has been suggested that these pots, when used for cooking, had been pushed deep into fire-places below the level of the flames. Studies of whole pots show the mid-sections have been exposed to the greatest heat, bases and rims the least. The idea of partial burial for stability, and of repeated exposure of the mid-section to a surrounding fire during cooking, has generated the term 'secondary firing'.

Early Phase (*c.* 4,500–3,000 BC)

Decoration, becoming more eye-catching in the Chubu and Kanto area, varied from region to region throughout Japan. Very thick cord-marking and stick-grooving, frequently on the same vessel, spread from northern Tohoku to the Kanto region. In the Kanto, Chubu, Tohoku and Hokkaido regions, there appeared a herringbone cord-marked pattern which had precedents in a ladder form (or a series of checks) used on the Sekiyama (J13) and other types.

From about the middle of Early Jomon, stab-and-drag stick-grooving became popular in the Kanto and Chubu regions of Central Japan (J20). Nail-marking, a manifestation of Western Japan (but excluding Kyushu and the extreme south-west of Honshu) (J29) was also a characteristic of Eastern Japan Moroiso-type pots (J23).

Jar bases became flat, a characteristic initiated in the Kanto region (J13) and continued countrywide (other than in Kyushu) for the rest of the Jomon period, as cooking moved from outdoors to inside houses. A very few exceptions had rounded bases (J16, J18). Feet were occasionally raised (J15, J28).

Jars were mostly over 30cm high (some exceptional Moroiso jars reached heights of 70 to 80cm) with cylindrical walls of varying shape tapering toward the base. Slowly the range of pottery shapes grew. The advantages of jars for the storing of food became more widely appreciated. Wide-mouthed cooking- and storage-pots of relatively simple shape had almost completely dominated the first stages of Early Jomon, but bowls (J21) also came into household use during this phase. All mouths were wide. Rims were usually flared and sometimes thickened by a band of clay. A few jars have somewhat trumpet-like necks expanding over narrower bodies. Undulating rims were not unusual (J13, J22).

The early Ento Lower cylindrical shape (J17) tapered from a wide mouth with straightish sides to a somewhat smaller, flat base. Surfaces had full coverage with many varieties of fine to fairly coarse cord-marking, and with string-indenting around some rims. Later Ento Lower vessels extended the scope of decoration and developed a wide range of shapes including more flaring, undulating rims, some with heavy collars, some with bulging bodies. In the northern Tohoku region, towards the end of Early Jomon, a beautiful wood-grain pattern on some Ento Lower and Daigi 2B-type vessels was produced by cord-wrapped stick-marking. The pattern was continued into the early part of the Middle Jomon phase.

The Sekiyama and related types of the Kanto region incorporated fibre as a temper and had heavy cord-marking. This shows a clear relationship to the Ento style of Tohoku where the heavy cord-marking began earlier. Some Sekiyama type jars (J14, J15) of the Kanto region have well-made spouts. One style (J14) has a defined deep curve in the rim of its wide mouth, the other (J15) has a round spout protruding from the body. This very early introduction of the pouring spout was not widespread in Early Jomon but it appears that spouts were an indigenous invention, and perhaps the earliest in the world.

Middle Phase (*c.* 3,000–2,000 BC)

With the Middle Jomon phase came a dramatic transformation from emphasis on the utilitarian to powerful artistic expression. The most elaborately decorated jars probably met ritual and visual as well as more mundane requirements, although it seems unlikely that any pots in Japan served a primarily ornamental purpose before Late Jomon.

The Middle Jomon phase in Eastern Japan witnessed a spectacular but gradual evolution from the more modest Moroiso-type pottery of Early Jomon. Lavish application of heavy relief with castellations (J32, J33, J39, J53) was widespread and was accompanied on many rims by equally extravagant, unwieldy protuberances which must have been more for artistic effect than for function. Some of these rim adornments were so large, cumbersome and freely formed that although some may have served for hanging or carrying one doubts their utility. For example, some Umataka type vessels (C7, J52), a very localized descendant of the Katsuzaka type, had most dramatic, flame-style (kaen) rim decorations. This production was heavily concentrated in Niigata-ken, in the Chubu region. Smaller lugs may have been functional (J54, J59, J67) but larger handles were so ungainly that, like the ornate rims, their serviceability is doubtful. In contrast to the many flamboyant rims, other were level (J37, J38, J48, J64, J66) or undulated (J31b, J62).

Stark evidence of cultural change is offered by the sculptural representations that swarm around the rims of the Middle Jomon Katsuzaka family of pottery types. These are concrete manifestations of zoomorphic and anthropomorphic repertories that form a consistent iconography. They are accepted by many archaeologists as offering firm evidence of an ideology, and hence associated ritual.

Cord-marking was still common on at least part of the surface of almost all types east of the Japanese Alps. However, particularly in the Chubu region during early Middle Jomon, cord-marking was overshadowed by the flowering of applied relief, elaborate, heavy and of extravagant artistry, together with split-bamboo grooved and indented designs.

Prototypes of Late Jomon zoned cord-marking appeared. (This was a natural extension of imposing grooved lines over cord-marking, a device seen on many Kasori E pots.) Cord-marking was first applied all over the surface; zones were then marked out in shallow grooves, and the areas within smoothed out. The effect was to alternate textured and plain areas in various patterns.

The woodgrain pattern of cord-marking which had appeared towards the end of Early Jomon continued on Ento Upper and Daigi vessels of the Tohoku region. It is shown in two Shimpo-style jars (J31a, J31b), one lightly, the other heavily impressed.

The evolution of central Honshu styles from Early through Middle Jomon is clear in the Chubu region, centred in Nagano-ken around the slopes of Mount Yatsuga, south-east of Lake Suwa. This area appears to have started the elaborate styles which extended eventually from coast to coast across central Honshu from Niigata-ken to Chiba-ken. Until the early 1970s Japanese specialists gave primacy to the lavishly decorated pots which flourished in the Chubu region's mountainous inland. A great deal of excavation since then has shown that the largest finds throughout Middle Jomon were in the adjacent Kanto region. The rapid expansion of pottery production inland in the Chubu region during the first half of Middle Jomon was not reflected in Western Japan but was paralleled with similar growth nearby to the east in the Kanto region. Early in the phase the Katsuzaka and Atamadai types were dominant, giving way later to Kasori E. The diversity of designs and colour is seen when comparing the heavier, coarsely tempered, terracotta-coloured Katsuzaka type (J34/J47) with the Kasori E type (J64/J72). The lighter, less coarse Kasori E was more often tan, even yellowish. It had applied ridges but relied more on grooving and lower relief rather than heavy appliqué. Open spaces were obliquely cord-marked. To the north, pottery also expanded in the Tohoku region.

Throughout Middle Jomon, cooking-pots and jars for storing nuts and other food remained of prime importance but, in addition, there were many other shapes. These included large and small decorated bowls, plain rather shallow bowls, and vessels some of which were almost certainly 'incense burners' or as fat- (or grease-) burning lamps (J43–J45, J60).

Barrel shapes with heavy vertical grooves were arranged into three or more wide, prominent, horizontal segments (J34, Katsuzaka and J51, Tonai). One odd very small barrel (J47), instead of grooved ridges, is decorated with four circular discs (two sub-human faces and two simple spirals). In the Kanto and Chubu regions some vessels had human heads in their elaborate rim and body decorations (J46). They were variations of rare Early Jomon prototypes, and were mostly Katsuzaka. Symbolic snakes were briefly popular around rims or bodies (J49). However, although distinctive on Katsuzaka-related types, this more realistic representation proved less popular with other Jomon potters.

Also in Kanto and Chubu, some vessels were painted with an iron oxide before firing. The paint was applied without designs to wide surface areas, perhaps for ritual symbolism (bones for secondary interment were often painted red), or perhaps to reduce porosity. Decorative painted designs were very rare.

In Middle Jomon bases were universally flat and serviceably broad. Some vessels were very large, some very small, even miniature. Outward extending shoulders and wide longish necks like those of Kasori E had been not uncommon in earlier types like Katsuzaka. Although flat rims became more customary, a minority still undulated or were castellated, as the more sober and less sculptural Kasori E came into dominance towards the end of this dynamic phase.

Late Phase (*c.* 2,000–1,000 BC)

The flamboyant, asymmetrical, heavy, three-dimensional appliqués of Middle Jomon (particularly of the Kanto and Chubu regions) gave way in Late Jomon to symmetrical, refined, quietly attractive decoration with more subtle artistic appeal. There was an increase in the variety of styles and a striking contrast between superbly rendered ritual vessels on the one hand and, on the other hand, the more widely made utilitarian wares.

Zoned cord-marking became a distinctive feature. It developed into freely engraved zones of large spirals and curves that ran more or less vertically, or in oblique panels. Cords were thin and the marking almost delicate within sharply outlined areas. Almost every possible variation has been found from Hokkaido to Kyushu. Kyushu adopted cord-marking by about the middle of Late Jomon and cord-marking was, for the first and only time, a country-wide motif. However, Kyushu soon abandoned the technique.

Both grooves and relief decorations were occasionally straight, but more often in S-curves and related shapes. The decoration of some pouring vessels was almost exclusively linear, and restricted to parallel lines and narrow bands of cord-marking. Undecorated surface ares were getting larger, but shell-marked impressions and bands of horizontal incisions still encircled many bodies at the neck and waist. Occasionally figures were added to the decoration and, following Early and Middle Jomon precedents, human faces have been added to a number of Late Jomon vessels (J80).

Some vase-like Horinouchi 1 vessels (J74, J76) had incised ridges in large panels, just below the mid-point of the vessels. Rim projections were coordinated with the body decoration in systematic repetition. Horinouchi 2 (J75) was a stage of somewhat less refinement with little attempt to smooth around carelessly laid out areas, although some pots were thin-walled. It registered a change from vertically to horizontally arranged decoration. Horinouchi shapes increased in variety to include vessels on raised feet (J77), pouring vessels (J78, J79) and 'incense burners' (J80) some of which may have been 'oil' lamps.

The cord-marked decoration of Late Jomon Kasori B (J84/J97) was lightly impressed by short, fine cords. Kasori B1 had narrow, horizontal bands incised or cord-marked. Kasori B2 had large, curved, often incompleted zones with cord-marked areas and many Kasori B3 had cord-marking above and below indented parallel lines. Junctures were sometimes marked by raised bosses and the repeated motifs were carefully calculated to fit the size of the vessel.

Knobby projections encircled the rims of many Angyo 2 vessels (J103, J106). There were heavy lugs at junctures and the surfaces could be crowded with decoration. The walls of some Angyo pots were thin and hard. The clay was pure and usually slightly reddish to dark brown. Both the hardness and the change in colour indicate improvements in firing technique.

As in all previous phases, cooking and storage jars still predominated over all other vessels during Late Jomon. Shapes varied widely. Many small vessels appear to be intended for individual servings. Level rims remained standard (J73, J81/J84), but some, especially on bowls, undulated (J91, J92) or had small raised protrusions (J74, J76). Some were castellated (J96), as had been so popular during earlier phases, and other rims were corrugated (J97). Sides were usually straightish, tapering to narrow base, but many bodies bulged. Necks were normally wide, everted extensions of the bodies, but some necks were comparatively narrow, or even tall, straight and slim (J89, J98/J100). With rare, curved exceptions bases, though small, were flat. The raised foot became quite common (J77, J78, J80, J86, J87, J89/J91, J94, J102, J103, J105) and ranged from low to high. Stubby feet were occasionally added (J93).

Bowls took many shapes. Dishes, plates and cups had come into widespread use. Bottles with small mouths (J100) and other vessels used for liquids appeared. Some pouring vessels had the tubular spouts that had their roots in Early Jomon and have also been found from Middle Jomon excavations. By the Late phase protruding spouts were common (J78, J86/J88, J106, J108). They increased in length until the mid-stage of the Late phase but by the end of the phase many spouts had been drastically shortened.

Some pouring vessels, which appeared first as rare examples in the Middle Jomon, became more widely used. They look so like twentieth-century tea-pots that they conjure up visions of space invaders, or time slips from the modern world. Of these 'tea-pots', some had curved ceramic handles (J86), others had lugs to hold hands of rope or cane (J78, J88), and some were handleless (J108). The tea-bush is not indigenous to Japan, so tea was not a drink during the Jomon period. To account for the evolution of this distinctive shape, the Jomon almost certainly drank herbal or alcoholic beverages. Not many of these spouted vessels are found in a site so it seems they were mainly used for rituals rather than in everyday life.

A few vessels, apparently also used in rituals, had lids (J78, J79). Some on raised feet (J80, J90) could have been incense burners but, alternatively, could have served as lamps. The use of another odd vessel (J105) is hard to comprehend. It is classed as Angyo type from Chiba-ken in the Kanto region and could have been an incense burner. An unusual Shinchi-type spouted vessel (J108) with a well-executed surface design could also be an incense burner. This vessel has some resemblance to Chinese Han dynasty 'hill censers', but it far predates the Han period (*c.* 100 BC–AD 100).

Final Phase (*c.* 1,000–300 BC)

In Eastern Japan during the Final Jomon phase a profusion of Obora shapes (J109/J134) largely follow Late Jomon prototypes, but were more numerous, more varied, and often more complex and refined. Obora-type vessels exercised overwhelming influence on other types in Eastern Japan and, to a lesser extent, Western Japan. Elaborate and strongly excised decoration flourished, and (as in Late Jomon) heavy appliqué was seldom used. Zoned cord-marking and geometric patterns of deeply incised lines featuring cloud, spiral, S-shape, and other imaginative motifs made by carving or erasure, added to the older designs. The undersides of many bowls were ornately decorated (J128, J129). While beautiful embellishment abounded, less decorated household pots were, of course, more usual.

Black surfaces were common. As well as burnishing, which was widely practised, some vessels were painted after firing. In many cases, particularly in the East, a clear or reddish-brown lacquer was applied, perhaps to preserve the underlying paint. Such vessels could have been for ceremonial use.

Wide and small mouthed vessels, and jars and bowls on raised feet were all plentiful. So also were bowls with straight and curved sides. Some bases were flat but most were somewhat curved. Many rims were also flat, and it may be inferred from their shape that some could have taken lids. However, there were also corrugated rims (J115/J118, J132) whose broken outline would have impeded drinking or pouring. Spouts were shorter than during Late Jomon. The 'tea-pot' shape lost its modern look and was produced with typical Obora decoration.

In contrast to the evolution in Eastern Japan during Final Jomon, the decorations and shapes of vessels in Western Japan changed little other than in northwest Kyushu where a new style of less decorated pottery was slowly emerging with prototypes of the largely plain pottery of the next Yayoi period.

In the Kansai region of Western Japan around Nara-ken, Kashiwara-type pots (J135/J137) were related to the eastern Obora family. The Kashiwara type, however, in contrast to the evolution in other pars of the Kansai region, was coarse with a gritty texture. It had imprecise shapes with a minimum of surface finishing and was made from either dirty brown or grey volcanic clay.

The Shigasato type in Shiga-ken, Western Japan, showed links with Obora and Angyo 3 from Eastern Japan and also with the Kurotsuchi type of the Inland Sea (Kansai) region. There is no doubt that the Obora type was the culmination of the ten millennia of the Jomon pottery tradition, and was hardly affected by the continental modifications being experienced in Kyushu.

Dogu and Masks

As in China and Korea and other nearby countries, the pottery of Japan down the prehistoric ages is remarkable, with few exceptions, for its paucity of figurines, sculptured shapes, and other non-utilitarian ceramics. Perhaps the inhabitants of Japan were more concerned with this world, their gods natural objects. However, in the course of time, some not yet understood rituals seem to have required anthropomorphic figurines, called dogu, which portrayed human form in either an abstract or caricatured manner (C14, C15, J138/J151, J153). In addition there are occasional animal figures (J152); a few masks and solid tablets (J154); a sprinkling of jars with human and animal-like decoration; and, as decoration or status symbols, some ceramic beads and pendants. There appear to have been few, if any, ceramic toys.

The earliest dogu have been found in village sites in the central Honshu mountains and Ibaragi-ken accompanying cord-marked pottery of the middle of the Initial Jomon phase (Kobayashi and Komei, 1984). Their extremely crude, rather plaque-like, featureless torsos have slight projections for heads, arms and legs. Little clay lumps on their chests indicate female breasts.

Dogu, more carefully made, appear again in the archaeological record in the latter half of the Early Jomon phase. Continuity with the first dogu is unknown, but they also were grotesque renditions of human forms, as were those that followed in later phases.

Dogu of Middle Jomon phase (J138) have been found in the Kanto region along with Moroiso style pottery and also in the Tohoku region and the southern part of Hokkaido.

The Middle Jomon phase figurines became more numerous and more recognizably human, with more noticeable protuberances for heads, arms and legs. Most are obviously female with small, rarely pendulous, breasts. A standard swollen abdomen makes most appear conspicuously pregnant and suggests that they symbolized fertility beliefs, but their role is not yet clearly understood. Specifically male characteristics are not obvious although some dogu may represent males. A few have somewhat catlike features (J138).

Dogu composed of two human forms are extremely rare. Though often heavily and artistically decorated, dogu seldom depict action or gestures. Almost all dogu have the appearance of standing, and crouched ones (J142) are uncommon. No signs of cult-orientation have yet been found, but these effigies were obviously of some importance in rituals or ceremonies. Dogu were often painted red as were human bones for secondary interment.

Dogu are almost never found intact. There is still considerable speculation as to why they were intentionally broken before being buried or discarded. The breaking could have been intended to let the spirit out from the break at the neck, back, arm or leg; or show that the dogu had been disposed of as it had no further use. Alternatively, the Jomon could have practised, as some people still do, magical rituals of transferring by incantation the pain or disturbance in a patient's body to the same part of a cult object and then breaking the object. It has also been suggested as one other possibility that the practice of making and then breaking of pregnant figurines was a ritual attempt to limit population growth. In early Middle Jomon, the Kanto/Chubu population was growing rapidly. A great increase in the number of dogu corresponds with the peak of Middle Jomon population, but dogu continued to be made in large quantities even while the population fell remarkably during the Late and Final Jomon phases.

Middle Jomon dogu were fired at low temperatures, their surfaces often crumbly. Late and Final Jomon figurines were higher fired with thinner walls made from better clay. From Late Jomon, dogu faces were rendered in caricatured detail (C14, C15, J139, J151, J153). In the Kanto and adjoining regions, some feet and arms and then toes and fingers became clearly defined. During Late Jomon the making and use of dogu figurines, popular in Eastern Japan, spread into Western Japan and, for the first time, Kyushu. They disappeared in Kyushu by the end of Late Jomon. Elsewhere in the west they lingered a little, but they are not found there after the latter half of Final Jomon.

At all times, variety rather than uniformity was normal. They are often found individually but large numbers (sometimes hundreds) are also discovered in single sites. So far the numbers excavated from comparable sites are highly variable. They were not buried in a fixed spot. There seems to be no indication of ground hallowed for their interment. Although the occasional dogu has been found in places set aside for rituals, such finds are exceptional.

Nagamine (1986:256) makes a distinction between standing and stylized dogu. She says that dogu were

> (1) the realistic or representational standing human figure, which also includes figures lying on their backs, and (2) the abstract human figure, with stylized (abbreviated) facial features, heads, arms or legs . . . Stylized figurines appeared as the forerunner of the standing form, but even after the appearance of the standing form of figurine and its development in later years, the stylized form remained in use, developing its own characteristics. Moreover, stylized figurines were more popular than standing figurines and dominated throughout the Jomon period . . . The stylized form was made with the full intention of representing the entire human body.

The dogu died away in the Kanto region in the middle of Final Jomon. Conversely, in northern Tohoku dogu reached their peak. They were much larger in size as well as more numerous than the figurines of earlier times and other regions. Outstanding among these Tohoku dogu are black, burnished, hollow figures with goggle eyes, sometimes called 'spacemen' (J139). The last flowering of elaborate decoration showed a high degree of technical skill and artistic refinement, as might be expected in the area which produced the Obora style of pottery. Dogu faded away with the Jomon culture.

A few other surviving ceramic objects must also have been used in long-forgotten rituals. They include, after about 2,000 BC, solid, flattish, ceramic, plaque-type dogu (J154) called doban. They became widespread but declined and then disappeared during Final Jomon.

A small number of ceramic artefacts in the shapes of animals (J152), turtles and insects were made, mostly in Eastern Japan during Late and Final Jomon.

Face-sized masks began to appear in Late and disappeared in Final Jomon. Compared with the hundreds of dogu, very few masks (only about twenty to date) have so far been found in all Japan. Of these, most are from the Tohoku region but at least one is from Hokkaido (the Mamachi site, Chitose-shi) another from the Kansai region (Butsunami site, Izumi-shi, Osaka-fu), and another (C16) from Saitama-ken, Kanto region. The purpose of these masks, dated as Final Jomon, remains unknown as there is no direct evidence for interpreting their use. They are widely distributed, but at the same time extremely rare.

Termination of the Jomon Period – Commencement of the Yayoi and Epi-Jomon Periods

The Jomon period did not end suddenly as the result of war or dramatic events. Historians widely accept *c.* 300 BC as a date to mark the end of the Jomon hunting-fishing-gathering culture, the adoption of wet-rice agriculture, and the use of metals. The same approximate date is also widely quoted for the termination of the Jomon pottery period and the commencement of the Yayoi period. However, scientific tests now give the start of the pottery transition as between 700 and 500 BC in Western Japan.

There is room to doubt that the Jomon people cultivated grain crops, even primitively, at any time until nearly the end of the Jomon period when rice cultivation was begun in Kyushu. The presence of any species of wild rice in Japan has not been confirmed. Rice cultivation appears to have been introduced to Japan during the end of the Late, or early in the Final Jomon phases, and brought with it the beginnings of fundamental change in the economy, the culture and the pottery.

The growing of rice came from contact with the Asian mainland. The stone implements, and the rice itself, derived originally from the lower Changjiang valley in China, where rice cultivation is reported from the Hemudu culture of the fifth millennium BC. Excavations in Japan and Korea show that the first rice and tools found in western Kyushu are almost identical to those of Korea of the same, or possibly a little earlier, date. There is a widespread assumption, but no evidence, that the rice was introduced to Japan from Korean. The first rice in Korea is found in the south. It definitely had not come from North China overland to Korea. Some archaeologists believe that rice was brought from the east coast of China to Korea and to Japan about the same time. This appears to be a valid possibility.

In Japan the earliest traces of rice-pollen, placed at about 1,200 BC (Tsukada,

1986:48), have been discovered at Itazuke, Fukuoka-ken, Kyushu. At Nabatake, not far from Itazuke, the earliest evidence of rice cultivation has been found – paddy fields, drainage ditches, wooden piles, stone reaping knives and carbonized rice grains. The earliest Nabatake stratum has been dated to 1,080 ± BC (Higuchi, 1986:123). Similar evidence of cultivation, dated a little later, has also been found at Itazuke with Jomon Yuusu-type pottery dated to about 900 BC (Higuchi 1986:123). The Itazuke level above this, about 800 BC, contained both Jomon Yuusu-type and Itazuke-type pottery which can be classed as Early Yayoi. The two types have so much in common that not all archaeologists can distinguish a difference.

Until 1985 the earliest recorded evidence of rice cultivation in Japan was limited to northern Kyushu. Recent excavations at the Mure site, Ibaraki-shi, Osaka City have revealed the remains of paddy fields of about Final Jomon to Early Yayoi date, only a few centuries after the earliest rice in Kyushu. It would seem that, at this very early date, a group with rice-cultivation techniques ventured on from Kyushu overland, or through the Inland Sea, to the Kansai region, the rich plains in mid-Honshu. Whether or not one postulates the migration of a new people or merely the acceptance of a new way of life, rice-farming certainly spread fast throughout most of the evergreen sub-tropical forest zone east and west of the Japan Alps. Within about a century of Itazuke type (Early Yayoi) pottery, rice farming appears to have been established in most regions west of the Alps, and Ongagawa type (second oldest Yayoi) pottery has recently been identified (controversially) in sites all along the Sea of Japan coast to Aomori in the northern extreme of Honshu. Conversely, rice-based agriculture does not seem to have gained acceptance throughout the eastern and especially north-eastern regions for several centuries after if became dominant in the west. The conclusion of most archaeologists is that the hunter-gatherer-fisher way of life was still viable along the seaboard of Eastern Japan, where the Jomon fishermen continued to exploit the rich resources of the Pacific Ocean.

It must be emphasized that Japan was not by any stretch of the imagination a homogeneous country during prehistoric times. Rice cultivation and the Yayoi culture had not effectively penetrated the Kanto region until the beginning of the Middle Yayoi period (c. 100 BC). Jomon pottery continued to be made in many regions long into the Yayoi period. In fact cord-marking and other Jomon decoration continued in many areas during Late Yayoi times (c. AD 100–300). A culture in Hokkaido called Epi-Jomon spread south briefly into northern Tohoku during Late Yayoi, and continued in the north until the late fifth or early sixth centuries AD and, in the Hokkaido region, well into the seventh century AD. However, at present, Jomon-style pottery produced during Yayoi calendar years is named Yayoi. There seems good reason to extend the Epi-Jomon nomenclature to all Jomon-style vessels made in remote areas during Yayoi years and to limit the Yayoi name to Yayoi-style pots. In naming pottery types, style could well be given priority over calendar dates, but this is not the present convention.

Until the end of the Jomon period, after about ten thousand years, the technology of pottery production had changed very little. As far as is known, Jomon wares were still fired in the open as no kiln structure has ever been excavated. Elsewhere in Asia, particularly in China, enclosed kilns had been used for thousands of years before the technique was finally adopted in Japan about the end of the Yayoi period.

Long before 300 BC, other innovations such as the potter's wheel, high-fired stoneware, and glaze had gained neighbouring China an unchallenged lead in the world of ceramic technology. By contrast the contemporary potters of the Final Jomon wares continued at their traditional level of technology, a level appropriate to the needs of hunter-gatherers and emerging agriculturalists. Whether one sees this as stagnation or stability, it is obvious that technology is not the only criterion of achievement. Even by the standards of today, the potters who created the best of the Obora wares deployed unsurpassed levels of skill and artistry.

As already mentioned, the transition from Jomon to the Yayoi period is usually dated to about 300 BC when both bronze and iron were first imported along with other evidence of mainland contact. However, the long-established belief that this was also the time when wet-rice agriculture first appeared is now being abandoned in the light of the early dates for Itazuke and other sites. Also in question is the precise date for the transition in ceramics from the Jomon pottery of hunter-gatherers to the Yayoi pottery of rice-farmers. About 600 BC there is a strong evidence of regional change in Kyushu. However, the generally accepted 300 BC may be an appropriate date for the ending of the Jomon pottery period as the new Yayoi pottery did not reach the main island of Honshu earlier and, as mentioned previously, Jomon pottery still held sway in Eastern Japan for many centuries after 300 BC.

Of Jomon pots N.G. Munro, a pioneer British archaeologist who excavated a shell-mound near Yokohama in 1906, wrote (1908:166 italics added):

> Although this pottery is never turned on the wheel and lacks the regularity of form attainable only by that process, it is the less untrammelled and roams into lavish conceptions of form and decoration, probably unsurpassed in any place or time. *The artistic talent of later Japan was rooted in the prehistoric past.*

More recently, Fujio Koyama (1973:21), perhaps thinking of Katsuzaka and Obora types, has also written:

> They are now eagerly sought after, especially by admirers of modern art. There is an air of profound mystery about these ancient pots, which, with their elaborate and strange patterns, some deeply etched and others applied in relief with rolls of clay, are filled with a wonderful vigour and a barbaric strength that was never again to be matched by any of the pottery of later ages.

As the foregoing pages have shown, the ceramic vessels of the past were never independent of their social context. The lifeway in which they functioned gave them meaning. Ceramics collectors can, of course, claim that archaeologists miss a great deal if they do not appreciate the visual beauty and the 'feel' of the vessels. Jomon pottery can be viewed from the stance of both ceramics collectors and archaeologists. Koyama expresses above the views of an accomplished potter, but a potter who was also an archaeologist and a collector. In all these roles he was attracted to Jomon wares as objects of beauty – a beauty which transcends their function for everyday use.

End Notes

1   In this book the term pottery, with one exception, follows Margaret Medley's definition (1976:13):

> It is essential in the first place to understand that pottery is a generic term. It is the name for the product of the potter, whatever its form, or distinctive material. Thus it applies without exception to all ceramic wares and comprehends earthenware, stoneware, porcelain and fritware, although we are not concerned with this last type in East Asian pottery.

The exception to the broad definition is that, in this book, the term 'pottery' excludes fired clay figurines which are discussed only in a separate chapter, Dogu and Masks.

2   It has been generally and somewhat vaguely believed in Korea that Korean Neolithic comb-pattern pottery had a Euro-Siberian origin. Kim has written (1986:23) that raised decoration points to a southern origin while mouth-rim decoration and pointed bases appear to belong to a pottery tradition found widely throughout the Siberian steppe. However, as Kim himself reports in the same book (p. 130), the Siberian origin view is 'challenged by a series of new radiocarbon dates, Amsa-dong 4,280–4,100 BC and Tongsam-dong 4,040–3,870 BC, which make it difficult to associate the Korean pottery with a Siberian counterpart because the latter is younger at least by one millennium than the Korean pottery.'

Kim believes that the earliest Siberian, or Soviet Maritime Provinces, pottery is no earlier than *c.* 4,000 BC, very much later than the earliest Korean. Although some very ancient Siberian sherds appear to have been found, a lack of evidence of continuity supports Kim's opinion. However, the indications of pottery contacts between the Soviet Maritime Provinces and Hokkaido could imply an extension southward from Siberia to north-eastern Korea about 6,000 BC. A lack of material from excavations in the USSR makes both opinions tentative. On the other hand, early comb-pattern Korean pottery shows considerable similarity to contemporary pottery in Kyushu.

Im (1984:20) writes that:

> Evidence of the earliest pottery making in Korea seems to have existed in the east coast and in the south coast, as represented by Sop'ohang Phase 1, Osan-ri Level V (B7/9) and Tongsam-dong Phase 1, sometime between *c.* 6,000 to 5,000 BC. Potteries from the east coast are earlier than any of the U- or V-shaped ones from the west coast. Sometime during the fifth millennium BC, probably in the early half (i.e. between 5,000 to 4,500 BC) 'classic' V-shaped comb-pattern potteries for the first time appeared in the west coast. In the east coast, earlier potteries were continually made, and in the south coast, potteries with thumb-impression decoration flourished.

We should note that, in a table of radiocarbon dates that Im appended to the same paper (p. 21), he records the following as the oldest pottery dates:

Osan-ri, 7,261 ± 120 BP KSU515 (about 5,350 BC); Tongsam-dong 5,890 ± 140 BP GX0378 (recalibrated 5,000–4,590 BC); Amsa-dong (west coast) 6,230 ± 110 BP AMS-N (recalibrated 5,280–5,050 BC.

The north-east coast site at Osan-ri sits on top of coastal sand-dunes developed around a bay which, after sand-bars formed, became a lake. The dunes today have been stabilized by covering vegetation. Three cultural horizons have been identified. From the lowest post-Pleistocene horizon seven radiocarbon dates have been obtained which indicated its age to be between about 6,000 BC and about 4,500 BC (Im, 1987:801). Obsidian for tools was brought from Mount Paektu near the northern border of Korea. Artefacts reveal an economy that relied on gathering and deep-sea fishing.

Sop'ohang shell-mound is a well stratified site at Kulp'o-ri, Unggi on the north-east coast. Although no absolute dates are available, this is partly compensated for by the radiocarbon dates from Osan-ri where the lowermost layers revealed pottery with decoration comparable to that of Sop'ohang. This may indicate that the pottery ages were similar (Im, 1987:18). On the other hand Kim (1986:32) dates Sop'ohang as about 4,000–2,500 BC.

The Tongsam-dong shell-mound, located on the south-eastern shore of Yong-do island just off Pusan, on the south-eastern tip of the Korean peninsula, faces the Tsushima Strait which separated Korea and Japan. Its three main layers (Kim, 1986) testify to a long period of occupation. Tongsam-dong is near the closest point between the Korean peninsula and the north-west coast of Kyushu. The intervening Tsushima Strait is notorious for its rough waters, but there is abundant evidence that the people who piled up the Tongsam-dong shell-mound were experienced fishermen with seaworthy boats. Obsidian flakes at all levels are thought to have come from well known quarries in western Kyushu. Jomon sherds from Kyushu are also found in all Tongsam-dong levels. That there was some trade with Japan, probably two-way and perhaps as early as about the sixth millennium BC, is undoubted but no evidence of Korean pottery of this period has yet been found in Japan.

Korea's early pottery has been characterized by, and named, 'comb-pattern'. This pattern is typical on pottery found in sites on the west coast of the peninsula. However, older, 'Pre-comb' or 'Proto-comb' wares have been excavated on the east and south-east coast below comb-pattern vessels. These earliest potteries are referred to as 'Mouth-rim decorated' (agari-muni), 'raised (appliqué)' (tod-muni) and 'Tongsam-dong plain' (Kim, 1986:23, 80). The mouth-rim and raised decoration vessels had flat bases (Kim, 1986:81–2) distinctively different from most Tongsam-dong plain, and the later comb-pattern wares, all of which had U- or V-shaped bases.

The earliest north-east coast flat-bottomed pottery was tempered with coarse-grain sand with the occasional inclusion of powdered shell. Typically, walls were about 7 millimetres thick and the colour was dark brown. Obviously, this 'plain' pottery had little or no decoration. When present it was usually limited to short, parallel incisions on rims, occasionally extended to the upper half of the body. The earliest west coast (Amsa-dong) comb-pattern U- or V-shaped pottery was tempered with mica, talc and asbestos. Decoration was slant and parallel jammed lines made by impression and incision on the rim, and rows of herring-bone pattern on the body.

3   Tsuboi (and some other writers) give BP dates. For ease of comparison, their figures have been reduced by around 2,000 years.

Some archaeologists persist with the 'short chronology', even in recent English language publications.

In an article, 'The Study of late Early Jomon culture in the Tone river area', *Windows on the Japanese Past* (1986:445), to support his own chronology Masae Nishimura published a table from which Table N.1 has been extracted. (The full table lists some other chronologies but these authors – B.S. Kraus, 1947; G.J. Groot, 1951; R.K. Beardsley, 1955 – are no longer active. All these chronologies are dated to the period before radiocarbon was used in Japan.)

Table N.1 Comparison of the main divisions of the Jomon period by different authors with those by the author (Nishimura) in 1967

Periods	M. Nishimura (1967) (BC)	J.E. Kidder (1959) (BC)	Radiocarbon dates (BP)
1 Sosoki	c. 2,500	–	$12,165 \pm 600$; $9,450 \pm 400$
2 Soki	c. 2,100	c. 4,500	$8,400 \pm 350$; $7,680 \pm 200$
3 Zenki	c. 1,700	c. 3,700	$5,100 \pm 400$
4 Chuki	c. 1,300	c. 3,000	$4,850 \pm 270$; $3,825 \pm 175$
5 Koki	c. 900	c. 2,000	$3,230 \pm 160$; $2,870 \pm 250$
6 Banki	c. 500	c. 1,000	$2,800 \pm 600$ $2,870 \pm 250$

In reviewing Nishimura's paper Kidder has commented:

> The author uses dates from my *Japan Before Buddhism* (1959) for the Jomon period to support his 'short chronology'. This book was written before the early Natsushima shell-mound carbon-14 determinations came out, though in the same year, and he ignores all later corrections, such as in my *Prehistoric Japanese Arts: Jomon Pottery* (1968) where charts and widely accepted dates are given. But this is the hazard of writing: One never knows what might be extracted.

4   Keally's sampling of sites and types so far excavated and reported on indicates the wide spread to choose from.

Incipient Jomon sites: Sempukuji (Nagasaki-ken); Kamino (Kanagawa-ken); Fukui (Nagasaki-ken); Muroya (Niigata-ken); Kosegasawa (Niigata-ken); and Kamikuroiwa (Ehime-ken), all (except Muroya) c. 10,000 BC.

Initial Jomon types: Natsushima (Kanagawa-ken) ($7,290 \pm 500$ BC) (treated as Incipient, not Initial by a large minority of archaeologists); Hanawadai (Ibaragi-ken) (c. 6,800 BC); Kojohama (Hokkaido) ($5,750 \pm 200$ BC); Akamido (Aomori-ken) ($5,160 \pm 120$ BC); Kayama (Kanagawa-ken) ($5,130 \pm 150$ BC).

Early Jomon types: Torihama (Fukui-ken) ($3,850 \pm 20$ BC); Uebo (Chiba-ken) ($3,570 \pm 140$ BC); Todoroki Lower (Kumamoto-ken) (4,000/3,700 BC); Sobata Lower (Kumamoto-ken) (3,700/3,000 BC); Kamo (Chiba-ken) ($3,150 \pm 400$ BC); Hamanasuno (Hokkaido) ($3,000 \pm 310$ BC).

Middle Jomon types: Katsuzaka (Kanagawa-ken) (c. 2,800 BC); Idojiri (Nagano-ken) (c. 2,800 BC); Togariishi (Nagano-ken) (c. 2,800 BC); Ubayama (Chiba-ken) ($2,563 \pm 300$ BC); Kasori E (Chiba-ken) ($2,500 \pm 110$ BC); Tokoro (Hokkaido) ($2,200 \pm 200$ BC); Todoroki Upper (Kumamoto-ken) ($2,010 \pm 130$ BC).

Late Jomon types: Horinouchi (Chiba-ken) ($1,930 \pm 150$ BC); Oyu (Akita-ken) (1,730 BC); Tsukumo (Okayama-ken) (not dated); Sobata Upper (Kumamoto-ken) ($1,350 \pm 125$ BC); Ishigami (Saitama-ken) ($1,140 \pm 122$ BC).

Final Jomon types: Shimpukuji (Saitama-ken) ($1,040 \pm 130$ BC); Obora and Kamegaoka (Aomori-ken) (c. 850 BC); Korekawa (Aomori-ken) (c. 850 BC); Yoshigo (Aichi-ken) (850 ± 600 BC); Itazuke (Fukuoka-ken) (610 ± 100 BC).

5   To emphasize the lack of unanimity in phase dating in recent works in English, Pearson (*Windows on the Japanese Past*, 1986:219) gives one series of divisions:

Incipient	11,000 to 7,500 BC;
Earliest	7,500 to 5,300 BC;
Early	5,300 to 3,600 BC;
Middle	3,600 to 2,500 BC;
Late	2,500 to 1,000 BC;
and Latest	1,000 to 300 BC.

However, Pearson also endorses a different series of dates (*The Rise of a Great Tradition*, 1990:15):

Incipient	10,500–8,000 BC;
Initial	8,000–5,000 BC;
Early	5,000–2,500 BC;
Middle	2,500–1,500 BC;
Late	1,500–1,000 BC
Final	1,000– 300 BC.

6   Matsuo Tsukada (1986:41) points to the charcoal of many forest fires, so many that he assumes they must have been started by human beings, and suggests that slash and burn agriculture might have occurred. He has also written (1986:41):

> During Early Jomon . . . sustained agriculture was still not practiced, staple crop plants were not indigenous and did not arrive in the archipelago until a much later time. Some archaeologists (e.g. Sasaki, 1971) believe that the finds of chipped stone axes and settlement patterns, i.e. the formation of villages, suggest that shifting agriculture was practiced as early as Middle Jomon. Cereal pollen is also found in lake Nojiri sediments dating back to 4,500 BP (*c.* 2,500 BC) although its species is not identified . . .
>
> The first continuance of millet-like pollen began *c.* 3,000 BP (*c.* 1,000 BC) . . . At the Ubuka site fossil buckwheat pollen grains were found in sediments dated from about 6,600 BP (*c.* 4,600 BC) to *c.* 4,000 BP (*c.* 2,000 BC) . . . It is unlikely that buckwheat was cultivated on the (Ukuba) bog because no peat disturbance was observed . . . Even after considerable search of the Ubuka sediments fossil buckwheat and cereal pollen grains were not found in levels between 4,000 and 2,000 BP (2,000 and 0 BC). It may be that agricultural activities were moved to sites at a distance from the bog.

7   Kim Won-Yong (1986:132, 160) quotes Lilian Sample (1974:110) as writing:

> It seems highly probable that the Tudo style (Korean) is a local development in which indigenous elements predominate. It is sufficiently convincing to conclude for the present time that the similarity between Todoroki (of Japan) and Mokto (of Tongsam-dong) is not a matter of direct cultural connection but of coincidence. However, should Sobata (of Japan) and Comb–pattern (of Korea) prove genetically connected, the dates would suggest it more likely that Sobata sparked the development of the strongly incised Comb–pattern of Korea rather than the reverse.

Kim then adds, 'Im Hyo-Jai, in his well received article (Im, 1982), upheld Sample's view on the origin of Comb–pattern pottery, but convincingly reversed her hypothesis on the relation between Sobata and Tudo pottery.'

8   Tatsuo Kobayashi's Styles

1	Ryusen-mon	2	Tsumegata-mon	3	Enkoh-mon
4	Tajo-mon	5	Yoriito-mon	6	Oshigata-mon
7	Kaigara Chinsen-mon	8	Hokkaido Hirazoko, Initial Jomon	9	Jokon-mon
10	Tokai Jokon-mon	11	Kyushu Kaigara-mon, Initial Jomon	12	Senokan-Hiragakoi
13	Jomon Sentei	14	Ujojo-mon	15	Hokkaido Oshigata-mon
16	Todoroki	17	Sobata	18	Ento Josoh
19	Daigi, Early Jomon	20	Usude Mu-mon	21	Kitashirakawa Kasoh
22	Moroiso	23	Ukishima/Okitsu	24	Jusanbodai
25	Hokutoh	26	Daigi, Middle Jomon	27	O(A)tamadai
28	Mujinazawa	29	Katsusaka	30	Kasori-E
31	Sori	32	Karakusa-mon	33	Kitakantoh Kasori-E
34	Goryogadai	35	Shinpo/Ninzaki	36	Kushidashin/Osugidani
37	Kamiyamada/Tenjinyama	38	Sakihata/Daigo	39	Kaen
40	Funamoto/Satogi	41	Adaka	42	Shomyoji

Tatsuo Kobayashi's Styles—*contd*

43	Nakatsu (Fukuda-K2)	44	Sanjuinaba	45	Kaya
46	Irie/Tokoshinai	47	Entai-mon	48	Ichiki/Isson
49	Horinouchi Kasori-B	50	Angyo	51	Kobutsuki
52	Gotenyama (Tsukikobu)	53	Ohsen-mon	54	Nishi Nihon Maken (Shigasato)
55	Kokushoku Maken	56	Surikeshi	57	Kamegaoka
58	Nusamae	59	Angyo, Final Jomon	60	Maeura
61	Shimizu Tennoyama	62	Hokuriku Banki	63	Fusen Amijo-mon
64	Ohtai-mon	65	Nanto Chinsen-mon	66	Zoku Jomon (Epi-Jomon)

English equivalents of Japanese names

Adaka	阿高	Hamada, Tamiko	浜田多美子
Akamido	赤御堂	Hamanasuno	ハマナス野
Akatsuki	暁	Hanamiyama	花見山
Angyo	安行	Hanawadai	花輪台
Angyo, Final Jomon	安行、晩期縄文	Hanazumi	花積
Aramichi	新道	Hashidate	橋立
Aso, Masaru	麻生優	Higashi Kushiro	東釧路
Atamadai (or Otamadai)	阿玉台	Higuchi, Takayasu	樋口隆康
Banki	晩期	Hokkaido	北海道
Butsunami	仏並	Hokkaido Hirazoko, Initial Jomon	北海道平底早期
Chinsenmon	沈線文	Hokkaido Oshigata-mon	北海道押型文
Chojagahara	長者ケ原	Hokuriku Banki	北陸晩期
Chubu	中部	Hokutoh	北筒
Chugoku	中国	Horinouchi	堀之内
Chuki	中期	Horinouchi Kasori-B	堀之内・加曽利－B
Daigi	大木	Ichiki-Issoh	市来・一湊
Daigi, Early Jomon	大木、前期縄文	Ichinosawa	一ノ沢
Daigi, Middle Jomon	大木、中期縄文	Idojiri	井戸尻
Daimaru	大丸	Igusa	井草
Dogu	土偶	Inaridai	稲荷台
Enkohmon	円孔文	Irie/Tokoshinai	入江・十腰内
Entai-mon	縁帯文	Ishigami	石神
Ento	円筒	Ishigoya	石小屋
Ento Josoh	円筒上層	Itazuke	板付
Epi-Jomon	続縄文	Iwashita	岩下
Fukumi-Suwayama	深見、諏訪山	Jokoh-mon	条痕文
Fukuda Kenji	福田健司	Jomon Sentei	縄文尖底
Fukui	福井	Jusanbodai	十三菩提
Fukura	吹浦	Kaen	火炎
Funamoto/Satogi	船元・里木	Kaigaramon	貝殻文
Fusen Amijo-mon	浮線網状文	Kaigara-chinsen-mon	貝殻沈線文
Gorvo	御領	Kaiten	回転
Gorvogadai	御領ケ台	kamegaoka	亀ケ岡
Gotenvama (Tsukikobu)	御殿山（突瘤）	Kamei, Masamichi	亀井正道
Goto, Kazutami	後藤和民	kamikuroiwa	上黒岩

Kamino	上野	Muroya	室谷
Kamiyamada/Tenjinyama	上山田・天神山	Nabatake	菜畑
Kamiwada-Joyama	上和田城山	Nagamine, Mitsukazu	永峯光一
Kamo	加茂	Nakamura, Kozaburo	中村光三郎
Kansai	関西	Nakatsu (Fukuda-K2)	中津（福田 K 2 ）
Kanto	関東	Nanto Chinsen-mon	南島沈線文
Karakusa-mon	唐草文	Nashikubo	梨久保
Kashiwara	橿原	Natsushima	夏島
Kasori-E and B	加曽利ーE、B	Nishikata, Yoko	西方洋子
Kato, Shimpei	加藤晋平	Nishimura, Masae	西村正衛
Katsuzaka (or Katsusaka)	勝坂	Nishi Nihon Maken (Shigasato)	西日本磨研（滋賀里）
Kayama	茅山		
Keya	気屋	Nojima	野島
Kikuchi, Toshihiko	菊池俊彦	Nunome	布目
Kinki	近畿	Nusamae	幣舞
Kitakantoh Kasori-E	北関東加曽利E	O(A) Tamadai	阿玉台
kitano, Kohei	北野耕平	Oatsu	押圧
Kitashirakawa	北白川	Obora	大洞
Kitashirakawa Kasoh	北白川下層	Oda, Shizuo	小田静夫
Kobayashi, Tatsuo	小林達雄	Odai-Yamamoto	大台山元
Kobutsuki	瘤付	Ogata, Yasushi	小片保
Kojihama	虎杖浜	Ohsen-mon	凹線文
Koki	後期	Ohtai-mon	凸帯文
Kokushoku Maken	黒色磨研	Okazaki, Takashi	岡崎敬
Korekawa	是川	Okinawa	沖縄
Kosegasawa	小瀬ケ沢	Okitsu	興津
Koyama, Fujio	小山富士夫	Omotodate	表館
Koyama, Shuzo	小山修三	Ondashi	押出
Kurotsuchi	黒土	Ongagawa	遠賀川
Kushidashin	串田新	Oshigatamon	押形文
Kushidashin/Osugidani	串田新・大杉谷	Oyu	大湯
Kushigatamon	櫛型文	Ryusenmon	流線文
Kyushu	九州	Ryusuimon	隆線文
	九州貝殻文、前期縄文	Sakihata/Daigo	咲畑・醍醐
Kyushu Kaigara-mon, Initial Jomon		Sanjuinaba	三十稲場
Maeura	前浦	Sekiyama	関山
Mamachi	ママチ	Sempukuji	泉福寺
Matsu, Akira	松井章	Senokan-hiragakoi	塞ノ神・平栫
Matsutani, Akiko	松谷暁子	Serizawa, Chosuke	芹沢長介
Megurogawa-togan	目黒川東岸	Shibokuchi	子母口
Mimanda	三万田	Shigasato	滋賀里
Monomidai	物見台	Shikoku	四国
Monzen	門前	Shimizu Tennoyama	清水天三山
Moroiso	諸磯	Shimono	下野
Mujinazawa	洛沢	Shimpukuji	真福寺
Mure	牟礼		

Shinchi	新地	Tsukidematsu	月出松
Shinpo/Ninzaki	新保・新崎	Tsukumo	津雲
Shiono, Hanjuro	塩野半十郎	Tsumegatamon	爪形文
Shomyoji	称名寺	Ubayama	姥山
Sobata	曽畑	Uebo	植房
Soki	早期	Ujojo-mon	羽状文
Sori	曽利	Ugashimadai	鵜ケ島台
Sosoki	草創期	Ukishima/Okitsu	浮島・興津
Suhihara, Sosuke	杉原荘介	Umataka	馬高
Sumiyoshicho	住吉町	Unoki	卯ノ木
Surikeshi	磨消	Usude mu-mon	薄手無文
Suzuki, Kimio	鈴木公雄	Watanabe, Makoto	渡辺誠
Tado	田戸	Yamanouchi, Sugao	山内清男
Tajo-mon	多縄文	Yamato-shi Education Committee	大和市教育委員会
Todoroki	轟	Yanagi, Soetsu	柳宗悦
Togariishi	尖石	Yanagimata	柳又
Tohoku	東北	Yayoi	弥生
Tokai Jokon-mon	東海条痕文	Yokohama-shi Education Committee	横浜市教育委員会
Tokoro	常呂	Yoriitomon	撚糸文
Tokoshinai	十腰内	Yoshigo	吉胡
Tonai	蒔内	Yusu	夜臼
Torihama	鳥浜	Yuzetsu	有舌ポイント
Toryumon	豆粒文	Zenki	前期
Tsuboi, Kiyotari	坪井清足	Zoku Jomon (Epi Jomon)	続縄文
Tsukada, Matsuo	塚田松雄		

9 The Yamato-shi Education Committee in 1986 published a detailed report on pottery sherds excavated two years earlier at the Kamino site and the Yokohama-shi Education Committee reported on their work also in 1986. Voluminous reports in Japanese record the extent of recent work being carried out on pre-ceramic and Jomon remains in Kanagawa-ken and throughout Japan.

10 The main types of Initial Jomon pottery could include:
Hokkaido: Memanbetsu, Akatsuki, Monomidai, Kojohama, Sumiyoshicho, Higashi Kushiro;
Northern Tōhoku: Hibakari, Shirahama, Kominatotai, Shimomatsu, Fukirizawa, Monomidai, Nozuki, Akamido;
Southern Tōhoku: Ichinosawa, Zao, Soyama, Daidera, Tsukinoki, Kamikawana;
Kanto: Igusa, Natsushima, Inaridai, Hanawadai, Mito, Tado, Shiboguchi, Nojima, Kayama;
Chubu: Sone, Ishigoya, Tatsuno, Tochihara, Kasubata, Uenoyama, Irimi, Unoki;
Kansai: Ogo, Kozanji, Ishiyama, Kishima;
Kyushu: Iwashita, Todoriki Lower.

11 In the Kanto region the Initial Jomon pottery sequence (following the type names and comments used in the Natsushima Shell-mound Report) was:

Natsushima layer	I	Daimaru, Igusa (Yoriitomon style, cord-marked)
	II	Natsushima (Yoriitomon)
	VII	Hanawadai (incised and shell-stamped, only a few cord-marked, some rouletting)
	III, IV	Tado (deep grooving, rough cord-marking)

V	Shiboguchi (shell-stamped and wrapped-stick cord-marked)
VI	Ugashimadai, Nojima, Kayama (incised, shell-streaked and scraped, nail-marked)
VII	Sekiyama (Early Jomon) (cord-marked, some small clay lump and nail-marking)

12 The main types of Early Jomon pots may include:

Hokkaido: Omagari, Ento Lower, Hamanasuno;

Tōhoku: Mushiri, Funairijima, Ruike, Fugoda, Kamikawana, Katsurajima, Ento Lower, Murohama, Daigi Lower, Ishigami;

Kanto: Sekiyama, Kikuna, Shimogumi, Nonaka, Futatsugi, Kurohama, Kamo, Moroiso, Hanazumi Lower, Okitsu, Uebo;

Chubu: Kijima, Kaminoki, Ario, Minomiohara, Uwappara, Harugamine, Fukura, Nunome;

Kansai: Azuchi, Kitashirakawa, Otoshiyama;

Western Honshu: Hajima, Isonomori, Hikozaki, Torihama;

Kyushu: Karatsu, Sobata, Todoroki Lower.

13 Middle Jomon pottery has been divided into types which include:

Hokkaido: Ento Upper (Hokkaido type), Tokoro;

Northern Tōhoku: Ento Upper, Saibana;

Southern Tōhoku: Nukazuka, Daigi Upper, Monzen;

Kanto: Goryogadai, Katsuzaka, Atamadai, Kasori E, Ubayama;

Chubu: Kyubei-one, Aramichi, Mujinazawa, Tonai, Omiyama, Idojiri, Umataka, Sori, Nashikubo, Togariishi;

Kansai: Daigo, Bannome, Sukumo, Shidehara, Funamoto, Satogi, Fukuda;

Kyushu: Ataka, Todoroki Upper, Nanpukuji.

14 Late Jomon type names can include:

Hokkaido: Wakimoto, Irie, Teine, Terugishi;

Northern Tōhoku: Oyu, Tokoshinai;

Southern Tōhoku: Miyato, Nishinohama, Shinchi;

Kanto: Shomyoji, Horinouchi, Kasori B, Takayagawa, Angyo 1 and 2, Ishigami, Iwai, Soya;

Chubu: Uenodan;

Kansai: Tenri, Kitashirakawa Upper, Ichijoji, Motosumiyoshiyama, Miyataki;

Western Honshu and Shikoku: Nakatsu, Fukuda, Hikozaki, Umatori, Shimomatsumo, Tsukumo, Hirose Upper, Arioka;

Kyushu: Kitakuneyama, Mitarai, Kanegasaki, Nishibira, Mimanda, Goryo.

15 Final Jomon types may be summarized as:

Hokkaido: Kaminokuni, Menasawa, Hinohama;

Tōhoku: Obora (Kamegaoka), Korekawa, Yahatazaki, Taira, Okamachi, Kuzusawa, Kenyoshi;

Kanto: Angyo Upper, Shimpukuji, Nishippara, Arami;

Chubu: Sano, Kori;

Kansai and Western Japan: Shiganosato, Kashiwara, Funabashi, Karako, Kurotsuchi, Hara, Takao, Hattantsubo, Nakamura, Irita, Nishikento, Yoshigo;

Kyushu: Kurokawa, Yamanotera, Yuusu, Itazuke.

Bibliography

AIKENS, C. Melvin and HIGUCHI, Takayasu (1982), *The Prehistory of Japan*, New York: Academic Press.

ALLCHIN, J. R. (1982), 'The Indian experience', in *Antiquity and Continuity*, Bangkok: Media Iransasia.

ALMAN, John H. (1960), 'Dusun pottery and Bajau pottery', *Sarawak Museum Journal*, vol. 9, no. 15–16 (new series).

AN Zhimin (1983), 'Carbon-14 dating and the Chinese Neolithic', in *31st International Congress of Human Sciences in Asia and North Africa (CISHAAN), Tokyo and Kyoto, 1983*.

AN Zhimin (1988), 'Archaeological research on Neolithic China', *Current Anthropology*, vol. 29, no. 5, December.

AN Zhimin (1989), 'Application of carbon-14 dating to the Early Neolithic in South China', *Quaternary Sciences*, 1989, 6, 2, English abstract 132–3.

ASO, Masaru (ed.) (1984), *Excavation Report of Sempukuji Cave*, Fukuoka Education Committee.

BARNES, Gina L. (assoc. ed.) (1986), 'Introduction: The Yayoi and Kofun', in *Windows on the Japanese Past*, Richard J. Pearson (ed.), Ann Arbor: University of Michigan.

BARNES, Gina L. (1986), 'The structure of Yayoi and Haji typologies', *Ibid*.

BEIJING Museum of Chinese History (eds) (1983), *7,000 Years of Chinese Civilization*, H. R. MacLean, (trans.), Milan: Amilcare Pizzi.

CHANG Kwang-chi (1983), 'Ancient Chinese civilization, origins and characteristics', *Ibid*.

CHANG Kwang-chi (1986), *The Archaeology of Ancient China* (4th rev. ed), New Haven: Yale University Press.

CLARK, Grahame (1977), *World Prehistory* (3rd rev. edn), Cambridge University Press.

DEREV'ANKO, A. P. (1990), *Palaeolithic of North Asia and the Problem of Ancient Migrations*, Novosibirsk: USSR Academy of Science, Siberian branch.

FIELD, Edward (1990), *Munro and the Mitsuzawa Shellmound*, BA thesis, University of London. (Unpublished: copies in Institute of Archaeology, London, and Haddon Library, Cambridge.)

GILL, Sam D. (1982), *Beyond the Primitive*, New Jersey: Prentice Hall.

GORMAN, Chester F. (1969) 'A pebble tool complex with early plant associations in S.E. Asia', *Science*, 14 February.

GOTO Kazutami (1980), *Jomon doki o tsukuro*, Tokyo: Chuo Koron.

HIGUCHI, Takayasu (1986), 'Relationships between Japan and Asia in ancient times', in *Windows on the Japanese Past*, Richard J. Pearson (ed.), Ann Arbor: University of Michigan.

HURLEY, William M. (1979), *Prehistoric Cordage*, Aldine Manuals on Archaeology, Washington: Tarazacum.

IKAWA-SMITH, Fumiko (1986), 'Late Pleistocene and Early Holocene technologies', in *Windows on the Japanese Past*, Richard J. Pearson (ed.), Ann Arbor: University of Michigan.

IM Hyo-Jai (1983), 'Radiocarbon dates of Korean Neolithic culture', in *31st International Congress of Human Sciences in Asia and North Africa (CISHAAN), Tokyo and Kyoto, 1983*.

IM Hyo-jai (1984) (in English), *Korea Journal*, vol. 24, no. 9, September (Seoul).

IM Hyo-jai (1987), 'Osan-ri: An early neolithic settlement of Korea', in Sambul Kim Wollyŏng (= Kim Won Yong), *Professor Sanbutsu Kingenru Memorial Lectures*, Seoul: Ishisha.

KATO Shimpei (1987), 'The Jomon culture', in *Recent Archaeological Discoveries in Japan*, Kiyotari Tsuboi (ed.), Paris: Unesco, and Tokyo: Toyo Bunko.

KEALLY, Charles T. and MUTO, Yasuhiro (1982), 'Jomon Jidai no nendai', in *Jomon bunka no kenkyu, 1, Jomonjin to sono Kankyo*, Tokyo: Yuzankaku.

KIDDER, J. Edward (1957), *The Jomon Pottery of Japan*, Ascona, Switzerland: Artibus Asiae.

KIDDER, J. Edward (1959), *Japan before Buddhism*, London: Thames & Hudson.

KIDDER, J. Edward (1965), *The Birth of Japanese Art*, London: Allen & Unwin, and New York: Praeger.

KIDDER, J. Edward (1968), *Prehistoric Japanese Arts: Jomon Pottery*, Tokyo: Kodansha International.

KIDDER, J. Edward (1974), 'Jar burials of the Middle Jomon period', in *Perspectives in Palaeoanthropology*, A.K. Ghosh (ed.), Calcutta: Mukhopadhyay.

KIDDER, J. Edward (1977), *Ancient Japan*, Oxford: Elsevier-Phaidon.

KIDDER, J. Edward (1979), 'The dating and the technology of the earliest pottery in Japan' (unpublished), Symposium on Origins of Agriculture and Metallurgy, East and West, University of Aarhus, Denmark, 1979.

KIDDER, J. Edward (1983), 'The earliest Jomon dwellings of the Hakeue site, Musashi-Koganei City', *Humanities* 4B, ICU Tokyo.

KIDDER, J. Edward (1984), *Guide to the Hachiro Yuasa Memorial Museum, I.C.U.* Tokyo: International Christian University.

KIKUCHI Toshihiku (1986), 'Continental culture and Hokkaido', in *Windows on the Japanese Past*, Richard J. Pearson (ed.), Ann Arbor: University of Michigan.

KIM Won-yong, OKAZAKI, Takashi, and HAN, Byongsam (1979), *Korean Prehistoric and Ancient Periods: World Ceramics, vol. 17*, Tokyo: Shogakukan.

KIM Won-yong (1986), *Art and Archaeology of Ancient Korea*, Seoul: Taekwan.

KITANO Kohei (1983), 'Ancient migration of crafts from Korea to Japan', *31st International Congress of Human Sciences in Asia and North Africa (CISHAAN), Tokyo and Kyoto. 1983*.

KOBAYASHI Tatsuo (assoc. ed.) (1977) (in Japanese), *Archaeological Treasures of Japan: Jomon, vol. 1*, Tokyo: Chuo Koron.

KOYABASHI Tatsuo (1983) (in Japanese), *Jomon Cultural Regions*, Tokyo: Yoshikawa Kobunkan.

KOBAYASHI Tatsuo (1988), Map of Jomon Regions, unpublished, held by Kobayashi, Tokyo, Kokugakuin University.

KOBAYASHI Tatsuo and KOMEI Masamichi (1984), *Jomon Clay Figurines and Haniwa: a Pageant of Japanese Ceramics*, Charles T. Keally (trans.), Tokyo: Nippon Toji Zenshu 3.

KOBAYASHI Tatsuo and OGAWARA Tadahiro (1988–9) (in Japanese), *Jomon doki taikan* (A survey of Jomon pottery), vols 1–4, Tokyo: Shogakukan.

KOYAMA Fujio (1973), *The Heritage of Japanese Ceramics*, John Figgess (trans.), Tokyo: Tankosha and New York: Weatherhill.

KOYAMA Shuzo (1978), 'Jomon subsistence and population, *Senri Ethnological Studies 2*, National Museum of Ethnology, Senri, Osaka.

LEACH, Bernard (1945), *A Potter's Book*, London: Faber and Faber.

MATSUI Akira and YAMAMOTO Tadano (1988) (not available commercially), *Japanese/English Dictionary of Japanese Archaeology*, Nara: National Cultural Properties Research Institute.

MEDLEY, Margaret (1976), *The Chinese Potter*, London: Phaidon.

MEDLEY, Margaret (1977), *A Handbook of Chinese Art*, London: Bell & Hyman.

MELLAART, James (1975), *The Neolithic of the Near East*, London: Thames & Hudson.

MELLAART, James (1981), 'The prehistoric pottery from the Neolithic to the beginning of EBIV (c. 7000–2500 BC)', in *The River Qoueiq, Northern Syria, and its Catchment*, John Matthers (ed.), BAR S98, (i), 1981, Oxford: BAR.

MELLAART, James (1988), unpublished paper held by Mellaart, London, British Institute of Archaeology.

MUNRO, Neil Gordon (1908), *Prehistoric Japan*, Yokohama: Published by the author.

NAGAMINE Mitsukazu (1986), 'Clay figurines and Jomon society', in *Windows on the Japanese Past*, Richard J. Pearson (ed.), Ann Arbor: University of Michigan.

NAKAMURA Kozaburo and OGATA, Yasushi (1964), *Muroya Cave, Niigata-ken*, Nagaoka Kagaku Hakubutsukan.

NISHIMURA Masae (1986), 'The study of the late Early Jomon culture in the Tone River area', in *Windows on the Japanese Past*, Richard Pearson (ed.), Ann Arbor: University of Michigan.

ODA Shizuo and KEALLY, Charles T. (1979), 'Japanese Palaeolithic cultural chronology' (unpublished), 14th Pacific Science Congress, Khabarovsk, USSR, 1979.

OKAZAKI Takashi (1983), 'The beginning of rice cultivation in Japan and its relationship to the Continent', in *31st International Congress of Human Sciences in Asia and North Africa (CISHAAN), Tokyo and Kyoto, 1983*.

PEARSON, Richard J. *et al.* (eds) (1986), *Windows on the Japanese Past*, Ann Arbor: University of Michigan.

PEARSON, Richard J. and UNDERHILL, Anne (1987), 'The Chinese Neolithic: Recent Trends in Research', *American Anthropologist*, 89(4).

PEARSON, Richard J. (1990), 'Jomon ceramics – Creative expression of affluent foragers', in *The Rise of a Tradition*, New York: Japan Society, and Tokyo: National Agency for Cultural Affairs.

RAWSON, Jessica (1980), *Ancient China*, London: British Museum Publications.

SAHARA Makoto (1981) (in Japanese), *Jomon doki taisei* (Complete guide to Jomon pottery), Tokyo: Kodansha.

SERIZAWA Chosuke (1976), 'The Stone Age of Japan', *Asian Perspectives*, vol. 19, no. 1, University of Hawaii.

SERIZAWA Chosuke and AKOSHIMA Kaoru (1983), 'The Emergence of Pottery in Japan and its Radiocarbon Age', *31st International Congress of Human Sciences in Asia and North Africa (CISHAAN), Tokyo and Kyoto, 1983*.

SERIZAWA Chosuke (1986), 'The Palaeolithic Age of Japan in the Context of East Asia', in *Windows on the Japanese Past*, Richard J. Pearson (ed.), Ann Arbor: University of Michigan.

SUGIHARA Sosuke and SERIZAWA Chosuke (1957) (in Japanese), 'The Shellmounds of the Earliest Jomon Culture at Natsushima, Kanagawa Prefecture, Japan', *Archaeology no. 2, Research Reports by the Faculty of Literature, Meiji University, Tokyo*.

TSUBOI Kiyotari (1977) (in Japanese), 'Chronology and characteristics by archaeological periods', in *Archaeological Treasures of Japan, vol. I, Jomon*, Charles T. Keally trans. for abstract in English, Tokyo: Chuo Koron.

TSUBOI Kiyotari (ed.) (1987), *Recent Archaeological Discoveries in Japan*, Gina L. Barnes, trans. Paris: Unesco, and Tokyo: Toyo Bunko.

TSUKADA Matsuo (1986), 'Vegetation in prehistoric Japan: the last 20,000 years', in *Windows on the Japanese Past*, Richard J. Pearson (ed.), Ann Arbor: University of Michigan.

VAINKER, S.J. (1991), *Chinese Pottery and Porcelain*, London: British Museum.

VALENSTEIN, Suzanne G. (1989), *A Handbook of Chinese Ceramics*, 2nd edn, rev., New York: Metropolitan Museum of Art.

WHITEHOUSE, Ruth D. (ed.), (1983), *The Macmillan Dictionary of Archaeology*, London: Macmillan.

WILDENHAIN, Marguerite (1962), *Pottery: Form and Expression*, New York: Reinhold.

YAMANOUCHI Sugao (1964) (in Japanese), *Nihon gendai bijitsu* (Primitive Arts of Japan), Tokyo: Kodansha.

YAMATO-SHI Education Committee (1986) (eds) (in Japanese), *Kamino Excavation Report*, Kanagawa: Yamato-shi Education Committee.

YANAGI Soetsu (1972), *The Unknown Craftsman*, Tokyo: Kodansha International.

YOKOHAMA-SHI Education Committee (1986) (eds) (in Japanese), *Yokohama-shi Excavation Report*, Yokohama: Education Committee.

C1 Incipient Jomon. Sempukuji site, Sasebo-shi, Nagasaki-ken. This reconstructed jar, believed to be one of the oldest pottery vessels recorded in the world, is illustrated in the *Excavation Report of the Sempukuji Cave*. The editor, Masaru Aso, has written: 'Radiometric dating of the site has been done through direct and indirect cross-checking of radiocarbon, thermoluminescence and obsidian fission-track age measurements all of which confirm to 10,000–8,500 BC age of this pottery style. There can be no doubt that pottery-making had its beginning in the microlithic culture.' Bean-lump decoration. Held by Sasebo-shi Board of Education, Nagasaki-ken. Height 22cm, mouth diameter 12cm.

C2 Incipient Jomon. Kamino Upper, Yamato-shi, Kanagawa-ken. Raised, parallel, horizontal ridges encircle the body above and below a broad band of four rows of diamond-shaped ridges. Held by Yamato-shi Board of Education, Kanagawa-ken. Height 22.0cm, mouth diameter 23.5cm.

C3 Initial Jomon. Yoriitomon style (second stage), Igusa type, Tama New Town site No. 99, Tokyo. Everted lip, straightish side, slightly curved base. Held by Tokyo-to Centre of Archaeology, Tokyo. Height 33.5cm, mouth diameter 27.0cm.

C4 Initial Jomon. Monomidai type, Takashira-naya site, Aomori-ken. Incised lines and shell-impressions are typical of the Initial phase. Height 30.8cm.

C5 Early Jomon. Ento Lower type. Shimizu-mukai site, Shizuoka-ken. Parallel, horizontal ridges below the lip, cord-marked. Flat bases. Held by Kokugakuin University Museum, Tokyo. Height of right-hand pot 37.0cm. Mouth diameter of right-hand pot 22.0cm.

C6 Early Jomon. Moroiso type, Ondashi site, Yamagata-ken. Lacquered bowl with holes pierced below the lip and curved lines below the lacquer coating. Held by Yamagata-ken Board of Education. Height 15cm, width 23.6cm.

C7 Middle Jomon. Kaen style, Umataka type, Okinohara, Niigata-ken. Heavily applied appliqué decoration around and above the shoulder and rim, vertical grooves on lower body. Held by Tsunanmachi Board of Education, Niigata-ken. Height 35.5cm.

C8a Larger. Middle Jomon. Kasori E type. Reddish with the upper part black. Incised lines encircle the expanded mouth of this large jar. Groups of cord-marking vertical from mouth to base, most of the surface plain. Noto peninsula, Ishikawa-ken. Height 47.3cm, mouth diameter 36.0cm (K173 Kenrick Collection, Tokyo).

C8b Smaller (C089) Middle Jomon. Kasori E type. Reddish buff. Lug above the flat rim with a collar decorated with a wavy encircling band above a toothed flange, the body cord-marked all over, the base flat. Mita, Ibaragi-ken. Height 21.0cm, mouth diameter 16.6cm (K089 Kenrick Collection, Tokyo).

C9 Middle Jomon. Katsuzaka type. This large, very heavily potted, utilitarian bowl is buff with blackish patches. The spreading, curved side, with rim inverted and inside grooved; a small, flat base, is undecorated. The plain surface is an unusual feature. It could have been made early or late in the phase. Ibaragi-ken. Height 10.0cm, diameter 26.5cm (K177 Kenrick Collection, Tokyo).

C10 Late Jomon. Horinouchi type. Aihara, Kanagawa-ken. Wide extruding mouth; curved grooving around upper side; lower side plain, side curving inward to large, flat base. Held by Kokugakuin University Museum, Tokyo. Height 19.5cm, mouth diameter 20.0cm.

C11   Late Jomon. Kasori B type bowl, black. Flat inverted, smoothed rim; side slightly curved inwards from the shoulder; body cord-marked, base grooved. Narita, Chiba-ken. Height 9.6cm, mouth diameter 14.8cm (K214 Kenrick Collection, Tokyo).

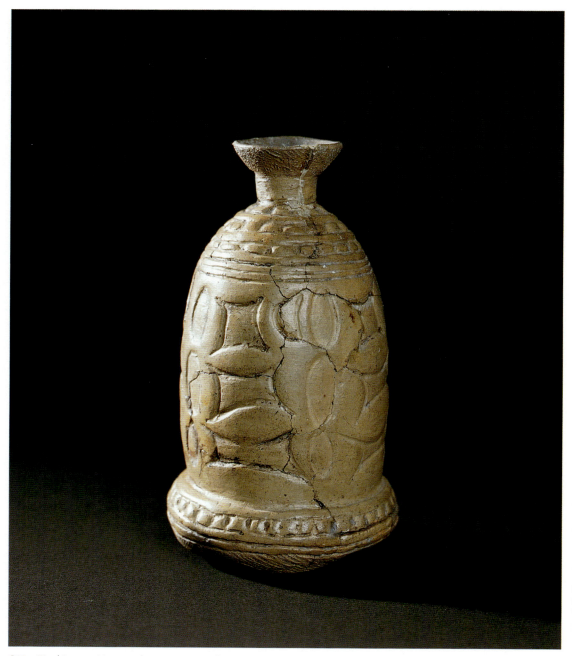

C12 Final Jomon. Kamegaoka type, Aomori-ken. Small everted mouth on short neck; shoulder and side deeply grooved; wide extending foot above slightly curved base. Held by Kokugakuin University Museum. Height 21.0cm, mouth diameter 5.0cm.

C13 Final Jomon. Obora B-C type. Light buff with some black. Bowl with serrated lip with three small extrusions; short, extruding neck; high, short shoulder receding to an extending, hollow foot; plain surface. Kamegaoka, Aomori-ken. Height 12.5cm, mouth diameter 13.3cm (K133 Kenrick Collection, Tokyo).

C14   Dogu. Late Jomon. Kasori site, Chiba-ken. Held by Kasori Shell-mound Museum, Chiba-ken. Height 14.85cm.

C15 Dogu. Final Jomon. Shakoki style. Taira, Aomori-ken. Top half of female figure with wide eyes and prominent breasts. Held by Fumi Inoue, Tokyo. Height 19.2cm.

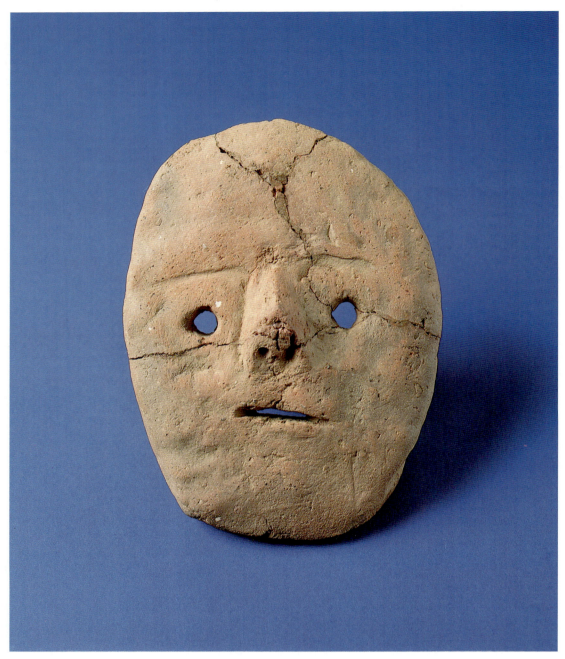

C16 Mask-like oval face. Late Jomon. Reddish/buff. Cut-out eyes and moulded nose. Kawagoe, Saitama-ken. Height 21.4cm, width 11.5cm (K213 Kenrick Collection, Tokyo).

China

J1a

J1b

J1c

These three vessels are among the oldest pottery yet found in North China. All are from Peiligang, radiocarbon dated no older than 6,500 BC (calibrated) as stated by Dr An Zhimin. All are brick-red.

J1a Fine clay, thinly potted, undecorated and smooth surfaced, with a medium-sized mouth, an upright neck, globular body, two small lugs on the shoulder and a slightly curved base. Height 14cm.

J1b Also fine clay, thinly potted with a smooth, undecorated surface, a wide-mouthed bowl on three short, protruding legs. Height 8cm.

J1c Coarse clay, heavily potted with a more upright, wide, extruding mouth, a bowl on three protruding legs with three horizontal rows of raised, applied bean-like lumps. Height 20.2cm. Photographs supplied by Dr An Zhimin, Institute of Archaeology, Chinese Academy of Social Sciences.

Korea

J1d

J1e

J1f

J1g

J1d A wide-mouthed bowl from the lowest level (sixth millennium BC, calibrated) Osanri, with three parallel rows of impressed short slant lines just below the rim the only decoration. The surface is polished. Colour red-brown, partly blackened by soot. Its curved, smooth side tapers to a small flat base with a slightly raised foot. Height 27.7cm, mouth diameter 37.5cm, base diameter 8.5cm, thickness 0.9cm.

J1e Another wide-mouthed bowl from Osanri with no decoration (plain), colour red-brown. Height 34cm, mouth diameter 51.4cm, base diameter 9.6cm, thickness 1.1cm.

J1f Also a wide-mouthed bowl from Osanri with six rows of applied linear relief encircling the body. The side also tapers to a flat base with a slightly raised foot. Height 16.5cm, mouth diameter 23.6cm.

J1g A jar with open mouth from Osanri, a lightly constricted neck, two well-formed lugs, a full body, a flat base. Diameter 11.3cm.

Incipient Jomon

J1h

J1h   Early Incipient Phase. Omotedate site. Rim serrations appear to have been made by thumb-nail impressions. Slightly extruding mouth. Upright sides encircled with parallel grooves covering the whole body above a pointed base. Rokkashomura, Aomori-ken. Height 30.15cm, diameter 22.0cm.

Incipient Jomon

J2

J4

J3

J5

J2   Muroya I type. The 1961 and 1962 excavations of the Muroya cave-shelter in Niigata-ken revealed the unexpected relationship of lightly cord-marked pottery with flat bottoms occurring in levels below pointed-bottom vessels. Small patches of cord-marking can be seen on this collared pot. The rim is cord-indented. Muroya cave, Niigata-ken. Height 21.0cm.

J3   Muroya I type. This seems to be the typical shape for vessels from the lower levels of Muroya cave. The walls are thin; the rim band projects above a slight constriction, but is not normally thickened. The rim carries most of the decoration, here probably a very primitive string-impressing; the band is outlined by cord-indentations. Muroya cave, Niigata-ken. Height 19.0cm.

J4   Muroya I type. The decoration is concentrated at the rim here in diagonal cord-marking. In this case the twisted fibres are of slightly different sizes, and the furrows alternate between shallow and deep. The edge of the rim is indented, perhaps by a cord. Muroya cave, Niigata-ken. Height 10.5cm.

J5   Muroya I type. The decoration of this rough-surfaced vessel is confined to the rim band, taking the form of a complicated variety of cord-marking and fine punctates around the two widest points. A hole, pressed out from the inside, is probably an overflow vent for liquids. Muroya cave, Niigata-ken. Height 14.0cm.

Initial Jomon

J6

J7

J8

J9

J6 Natsushima type. Pottery in the Kanto Plain at this stage served hardly any other purpose than for cooking, and size and shape were fairly standardized. This relative consistency may have been due to the contact between small groups of people who became acquainted with their neighbours' utensils. Natsushima, Kanagawa-ken. Height 25.1cm.

J7 Hanawadai type. The surface was smoothed with a hard object, leaving burnishing marks still visible, and is otherwise undecorated. The clay is quite fine. Sherds from this shell-mound may be plain, incised, scratched or string-impressed. Hanawadai, Ibaragi-ken. Height 19.8cm.

J8 Inaridai type. Probably the thickening of rims was believed to be a way of reducing cracking under the strain of constant use. The lip gave an advantage in picking up the vessel. Daimaru, Kanagawa-ken. height 28.2cm.

J9 Tado I type. In both the decoration and sharply pointed base this grooved and excised vessel is very close to the Tado I type of the Kanto Plain, especially of the Miura Peninsula. The surface here is far rougher. Some Tado I pottery bears red paint on the interior. Muroya cave, Niigata-ken. Height 30.5cm.

Initial Jomon

J10

J11

J12

J10   Unoki type. Oval and zigzag rouletted impressions in alternating bands weave an interesting surface pattern on this vessel. Most of the pot is a blackish brown, while the fragile lower part is a strong red. Carbonized food still encrusts the interior. Unoki, Niigata-ken. Height 23.0cm.

J11   Kayama type. The Kayama type is shell-scraped; the clay is coarse and copiously fibre-tempered. The walls are fairly thick, the bases flat or rounded. The slight peaks on the rim are not carefully co-ordinated with the decoration, which consists of heavy punctates in the zones formed by the incised zigzags and rim-collar line. Tobinodai, Chiba-ken. Height 27.0cm.

J12   Sumiyoshicho type. This shell-marked pot, probably imprinted with a scallop shell, has a far more exaggeratedly peaked rim than most pointed-bottom vessels. The walls are fairly straight, and characteristically northern. Sumiyoshicho, Hokkaido.

Early Jomon

J13

J14

J15

J16

J13   Sekiyama type. Bamboo-stick-marked patterns on the rim collar and herringbone cord-marking spreading characterize this type, as does the body and flat foot. This was a new shape in the Kanto area and was a practical effort toward functional improvements in the cooking-pot. Futatsugi, Chiba-ken. Height 35.0cm.

J14   Sekiyama type. With lip-spout to facilitate the emptying of the pot, the rim of this vessel has been enhanced by semicircular projections. The curved and diagonal stick-marked pattern on the upper half were superimposed on the oblique cord-marking. Asukayama Park, Tokyo. Height 33.0cm.

J15   Sekiyama type. Sekiyama-type pottery has a fairly consistent appearance. It occurs chiefly in the prefectures of Tokyo, Saitama and Chiba, and is more abundant than any of its predecessors in the Kanto Plain. First attempts at spouts are to be seen in this stage. Nishiyokono, Gumma-ken. Height 14.0cm.

J16   Nunome type. The site lies on a sandbank along the shore of the Kamisekigata (a swamp), and has yielded a single pottery type – named after the site – which is apparently a variant of the Ento types. The dense cord-marking is disposed in narrow registers. Nunome, Niigata-ken. Height 37.0cm.

Early Jomon

J17

J18

J19

J17 Ento Lower C type. Ento types are known for their extensive cord-marked surfaces, often displaying string-impressions in simple patterns near the rim. These types, with their dense cord-marking, which includes wood-grain, herringbone and other designs, graphically illustrate the variety of such decoration in contemporary use. Ichioji, Aomori-ken. Height 40.3cm.

J18 Hanazumi Lower type. Heavily cord-marked in alternating oblique bands produced by knotting and twisting the cords in the opposite directions, this vessel is much like Early Jomon pottery of east and north Japan. Its presence above the other types in the cave points to a very prolonged period of occupation. Muroya cave, Niigata-ken. Height 33.0cm.

J19 Hanazumi Lower type. Purely domestic ware of the Hanazumi Lower type has uneven walls, extensive cord-marking, and frequently a slightly raised base. The clay is fibre-tempered. Kikuna, Kanagawa-ken. Height 28.3cm.

Early Jomon

J20

J21

J22

J23

J20   Okitsu type. This exceptionally large vessel has been spoken of as a prototype for the big bowls of early Middle Jomon. Stick-marking and shell-imprinting, here rigidly horizontal, enhance the curves of the vessel and add to its clean-cut, functional appearance. Okitsu, Ibaragi-ken. Height 44.5cm.

J21   Moroiso A type. This is a typical Moroiso type bowl, bamboo-stick-marked and obliquely cord-marked. The cardinal Moroiso traits are found from the Kanto area to the Inland Sea, across the central mountains to Niigata, and as far north as Miyagi-ken. Variants appear even beyond these limits. Height 12.6cm.

J22   Moroiso A type. A cousin to J23, also with oval-shaped rim, the applied work on the piece provides only a thickened rim and minor other decoration. Stab-and-drag patterns are more interesting; lightly done cord-marking appears faintly in a few enclosed areas. Murayama, Gifu-ken. Height 32.0cm.

J23   Moroiso A type. Fortunately, enough was recovered for the upper two-thirds to be reconstructed. The Moroiso type ridges are much heavier than usual, and the arc-shaped parallel lines marked with the end of a split bamboo stick are only one notch above doodling. Murayama, Gifu-ken. Height 47.5cm.

Early Jomon

J24

J25

J26

J27

J24   Moroiso C (Kusabana) type. The last Moroiso type reflects a growing interest in the plastic decoration best seen in the Middle Jomon period. Cord-marking is largely ignored in favour of liberal stick-marking, and fibre-tempering is abandoned in favour of grit-tempering. Hanatoriyama, Yamanashi-ken. Height 22.4cm.

J25   Moroiso type. This tall, utilitarian jar has a wide open mouth, rim rising in two simple castellations, Fukushima-ken. Height 22.9cm (K226 Kenrick Collection, Tokyo).

J26   Moroiso type. Buff with large black patches. Wide mouth, flat lip, straight side tapering to a flat bottom. Combed, straight vertical lines on a plain surface. Hirakawa, Matsuda-shi, Chiba-ken. Height 20.3cm, mouth diameter 20.9cm (K208 Kenrick Collection, Tokyo).

J27   Moroiso type (or, possibly, Middle Jomon Kasori E). Reddish with black area. Wide mouth with slightly everted, formed lip. Straight side tapering to a large, flat bottom. Whole surface cord-marked. Fukushima-ken. Height 21.0cm, mouth diameter 18.3cm (K002 Kenrick Collection, Tokyo).

Early Jomon

J28

J29

J30

J31

J28   Fukura type. The thin, closely notched ridge, often occurring in parallel pairs and here resulting in a beaded effect, was widely used in the latest types of Early Jomon, such as Daigi 6, Jusanbodai and Otoshiyama, all distant relatives within the Moroiso family. The lower wall of this pot is much heat-reddened. Fukura, Yamagata-ken. Height 19.7cm.

J29   Kitashirakawa Lower 2 type. Illustrated here is the well known 'nail-marked' vessel that was found on the chest of 'earring-wearing' skeleton No. 3 at the Ko excavation in 1918. The site has more recently been dug for stratigraphic information. Ko, Osaka. Height 16.0cm.

J30 and **J31**   Sobata type. Usually round based, Sobata type pottery is widely scattered in western Kyushu and out into Tanegashima and Yakushima islands. Rather short, straight line grooving is customary. Sobata, Kumamoto-ken. Heights 37.0cm and 12.0cm.

Middle Jomon

J31a

J31b

J31a Early part of Middle Jomon, Shimpo style. Wood-grain, lightly impressed cord-marking following Ento and Daigi patterns. Extruded, serrated rim, wide, flat base. Mawaki site, Ishikawa-ken. Height 28.2cm.

J31b Early part of Middle Jomon, Shimpo style. Wood-grain cord-marking also following Ento and Daigi patterns. Undulating, serrated, rim and wide, flat base. Also from Mawaki site, Ishikawa-ken. Height 19.9cm.

Middle Jomon

J32

J33

J34

J35

J32   Atamadai 3 type. Atamadai's castellated rims are Jomon pottery's most extreme. They rise off a large, overhanging rim collar and are so ornate as to bring into question the essential usability of the vessel. The lower part received intense heat from a fireplace, beside which the pot was found. Tsukayama, Tokyo. Height 52.0cm.

J33   Atamadai type, similar to J32 but a little less ornate and with only three castellations. The lugs below the rim could have served as handles but the weight of the pot and the fragility of the lugs make this use doubtful. Ibaragi-ken. Height 49.5cm, mouth diameter 29.6cm.

J34   Katsuzaka 1 type. This is one of the smallest examples of the barrel-shaped vessels. The decoration on the lobes becomes simpler in descending order. The rim is not thickened, but has a wide groove cut into the inner wall. Nakahara, Tokyo. Height 12.8cm.

J35   Katsuzaka 2 type. Extensive split-bamboo stick-marking appears with applied strips; the former might have inspired the latter, or at least the chronological relationship suggests it. The surface here is flat for this type, and all decoration points to the fact that these potters concerned themselves chiefly with plastic form and variety in effect. Ushinuma, Tokyo. Height 59.0cm.

Middle Jomon

J36

J37

J38

J39

J36   Katsuzaka 2 type. Sites in west Tokyo, especially between Mitaka and Hachioji, have yielded magnificent Katsuzaka vessels, many virtually indistinguishable from pottery of the central mountains. The heavy appliqué is Chubu region derived; the cord-marking is more popular on vessels from the Kanto Plain. Nakahara, Tokyo. Height 35.5cm.

J37   Katsuzaka 2 type. One of the trimmer Katsuzaka shapes, the silhouette completely unbroken. The wavy (alternately notched) ridges are especially stressed here, and the zones are filled with spirals and the corners by three-pointed stars. Akitacho, Tokyo. Height 25.5cm.

J38   Katsuzaka type. Light buff rolled rim, straight side tapering to a reasonably large, flat base. Incised, curving design on upper body, lower half plain. Tsukuda, Saitama-ken. Height 33.5cm, mouth diameter 26.5cm (K200 Kenrick Collection, Tokyo).

J39   Katsuzaka 2 type. Katsuzaka vessels are of reddish clay; the clay often quite gritty, the walls thick. The cup rim is somewhat obscured here by the steep peaks, two of which resemble breaking waves. Panels outlined by notched ridges are the Katsuzaka trademark. Nakahara, Tokyo. Height 37.2cm.

Middle Jomon

J40

J41

J42

J43

J40 Katsuzaka type. Numerous pot handles found in large Middle Jomon sites prove that breakage was commonplace, and the functional use of elaborate handle-like projections had a very short time span. Such functional parts lent themselves too readily to extensive embellishment. Takikubo, Tokyo. Height 37.4cm.

J41 Katsuzaka type. This large pot, with restored base, retains a remarkably unbroken flatness on the surface for this type and time. Applied strips of clay on the body are bordered by cut-out ridges; the panels are either crosshatched or marked in a stab-and-drag manner. Parts of the rim are ruffled. Narahara, Tokyo. Height 80.0cm.

J42 Katsuzaka type. The decoration of the vessel here seems incoherent except as it gives ornamental effect to the handle and is used to avoid symmetry. Nakahara, Tokyo. Height 36.3cm.

J43 Katsuzaka 3 type. This kind of vessel was designed to be suspended. The whole 'incense burner' class has been a problem because such vessels have normally not been found with other pottery. One suggestion is that this is due to the fact that as lamps they were hung on beams, later falling haphazardly. Sakai, Yamanashi-ken. Height 21.0cm.

Middle Jomon

J44

J45

J46

J47

J44 Katsuzaka type. Yamanashi Prefecture's few 'lamps' are of the Katsuzaka type, like those of Nagano Prefecture, the cradle of this shape. These are flatter and more basket-like. Kuwakubo, Yamanashi-ken. Height 19.4cm.

J45 Katsuzaka (?) type. The 'incense burners' or lamps range from the most simple to the most elaborate. It is doubtful, however, that such differences represent a chronological or stylistic development. To some extent the potters were experimenting with both light-diffusing and suspension methods.

J46 Katsuzaka 1 type. The rodent-like head, with nose, slanted eyes and slight harelip, is typical of rim heads, but a strange aberration is its presence here on a bowl – in itself an oddly rounded shape for Katsuzaka – and on the wall rather than the rim. Sori, Nagano-ken. Height 11.4cm.

J47 Katsuzaka type. This little pot of miniature size seems to be one of the barrel-shaped vessels. It bears four circular discs, two with subhuman faces and two with simple spirals. The clay is coarse, the colour reddish with blackened areas. Sakai, Yamanashi-ken. Height 8.0cm.

Middle Jomon

J48

J49

J50

J51

J48   Nashikubo type. Early Middle Jomon frequently depends on extreme contrasts for dramatic effect, in this case a plain surface serves as background for finely stick-marked, rounded ridges, and there is an abnormal ratio of height to diameter. The lower part of the vessel was subjected to much heat. Karasawa, Nagano-ken. Height 30.0cm.

J49   Tonai type. The curved ridges on either side of the body have been called snakes by a number of archaeologists working with the Middle Jomon stage. Teruya Esaka has written that it may not be too much to suggest that all Middle Jomon decoration is snake-derived. Tonai, Nagano-ken. Height 37.0cm.

J50   Tonai 2 type. Heavy, piled-up appliqué may be rather extreme, yet in some cases it must have seemed imperative to keep the rim uncluttered. Why this was done is uncertain, but perhaps there were instances of fitted lids. Handles here are eye-like; other examples resemble ears. The horizontal tiers of relief, so common to the Katsuzaka family types, with irregular repetition of patterns, attract attention to the decoration but away from the vessel's shape. Tokuri, Nagano-ken. Height 47.0cm.

J51   Tonai type. This piece is built up in seven sections, including the rim. Such elaborately segmented shapes are unique to the earliest half of Middle Jomon. This pot was among more than ten vessels aligned in the centre of clustered pit-dwellings at this site. Tonai, Nagano-ken. Height 58.0cm.

Middle Jomon

J52

J53

J54

J55

J52 Umataka type. Giving vent to all artistic impulses, using clay pictorially, the potter fashioned a rich array of handle and rim details, heightening the artistic impact through the intricate play of light and shade. Tokushoji, Niigata-ken. Height 29.2cm.

J53 Umataka 1 type. The Umataka type seems to begin in a fairly orderly way, perhaps basing its decoration on the widespread Moroiso stick-marking style. The shape of both body and rim are not yet obliterated; inner surfaces are clean and smooth, yet the sculptural explosion is clearly imminent. Umataka, Niigata-ken. Height 29.7cm.

J54 Umataka type. The rim lip and the clay shapes like magatama (curved beads) on the rim are variations of orifice decoration of this type. Most typical is the meticulously executed ribbed surface and whirlpool configurations near the neck and flared mouth. Umataka, Niigata-ken. Height 25.0cm.

J55 Umataka type. The Umataka pottery type shades off from earlier into later Middle Jomon, an example of the latter being this fine, cord-marked bowl. Excision has produced accented decoration – less a characteristic of earlier examples – concentrated around rim peaks and on the exterior inturned curve of the body. Umataka, Niigata-ken. Height 11.0cm.

Middle Jomon

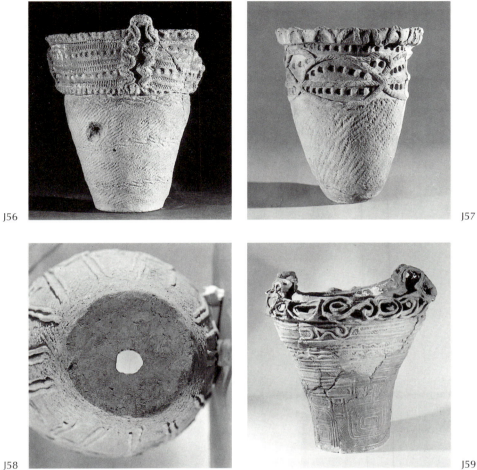

J56

J57

J58

J59

J56 Ento Upper B type. This is a very remarkable pot. Its most striking feature is the open, vertical, zigzag arrangement of clay strips resembling an oyster shell on the heavy rim collar. String-impressing can be seen in several places. Sannai, Aomori-ken. Height 24.7cm.

J57 Ento Upper B type. The people who made the early Ento types quite probably felt that they had arrived at an all-purpose shape. It changes little for centuries. Applied strips give a strong two-layer effect to the decoration. Ichioji, Aomori-ken. Height 18.0cm.

J58 Daigi 8B type. This burial jar, found with several others, has a small, roundish hole in the base. This hole is seen in several examples of burial pots. Tsunagi, Iwate-ken. Height 50.0cm.

J59 Daigi 7 type. In another cake-decoration style, an interesting feature is the way the decoration is scaled down from very high and thick at the rim to thin and almost flush with the surface at the foot. Oblique cord-marking covered the surface before the clay strips were applied. Ogonizawa, Yamagata-ken. Height 34.5cm.

Middle Jomon

J60

J61

J62

J63

J60 Idojiri type. Claimed to revolutionize views on Jomon 'incense burners', this handled bowl was lying apart from several other vessels in a pit-dwelling. It has remains of a black wick near the juncture of handle and body and a soot-covered interior, implying that it served as a lamp. Idojiri, Nagano-ken. Height 24.0cm.

J61 Idojiri II type. This astonishing vessel – on which ridges of triangular section were incised obliquely, outlined, then the outlines punched to further emphasize the ridges – shows the Atamadai type's appearance of sewn leather, the ridges resembling loosely hanging ropes. Tonai, Nagano-ken. Height 27.5cm.

J62 Monzen type. This was a cooking-pot whose bottom was ruined after considerable use. This type seems to be analogous to Daigi 8B, but it has been connected with Late Jomon through its gently waved peaks, early form of zoned cord-marking and vertical strips below the rim peaks. Monzen, Iwate-ken. Height 26.5cm.

J63 Sori type. One of the most perfectly formed of this type, most of which are above average in workmanship, its contrasts reflecting the discriminating taste of its maker, this piece has the size normally required of a burial pot at this time. Yamanashi-ken. Height 61.2cm.

110

Middle Jomon

J64

J65

J66

J67

J64   Kasori E type. Tall jar with a wide mouth and flat rim, contracting in a gentle curve to a slightly tapering straight side and flat base. Reddish, vertical grooves and fibre-tempered. Yamagata-ken. Height 21.7cm, mouth diameter 17.3cm (K165 Kenrick Collection, Tokyo).

J65   Kasori E type. Buff, partly blackened. Two small protuberances on the flat, ridged rim above two incised, wavy encircling lines. Extruding shoulder tapering to a flat base. Cord-marked over the whole body. Tsukuba, Ibaragi-ken. Height 31.9cm, mouth diameter 18.1cm (K149 Kenrick Collection, Tokyo).

J66   Kasori E type. Lightish buff. Flat rim. Slightly inverted collar with long, applied relief lines. Shoulder contracts in a straight line to mid-body then, below two raised encircling ridges, tapers to a flat base. Lower half restored. Nagaoka, Niigata-ken. Height 42.0cm, mouth diameter 33.0cm (K231 Kenrick Collection, Tokyo).

J67   Kasori E type. Buff. Three pierced ears above the flat rim, indented inside. Collared broad neck with grooves and heavy, applied oval relief design. The body with flowing grooves wide-spaced over the whole surface. Tsukuba, Ibaragi-ken. Height 37.2cm, mouth diameter 25.2cm (K126 Kenrick Collection, Tokyo).

Middle Jomon

J68

J69

J70

J71

J68 Kasori E3 type. An immense vessel, perhaps for storage purpose, it bears the early form of zoned cord-marking, at this stage utilizing relief effects of Middle Jomon to define the areas. In Late Jomon the zones run horizontally and are outlined, the ridges no longer being needed for this purpose. One, Gumma-ken. Height 56.0cm.

J69 Kasori E3 (Ubayama) type. Togariishi is the western-most point from which these large pots are found; Yamanashi Prefecture is their distribution centre. Magnificent, sweeping ornamental curves link the handles organically with the body decoration in an integration of functional parts with decoration known in few other types. Yosukeone, Nagano-ken. Height 53.5cm.

J70 Kasori E1 (Ubayama) type. A vessel with fan-shaped castellations was unearthed with this one. By the latter half of Middle Jomon the lug-shaped rim projections are an obvious survival of the extravagant earlier Middle Jomon rims. One, Gumma-ken. Height 8.0cm.

J71 Kasori E (Ubayama) type. Huge in capacity, displaying paired 'fins' on the rim and one of the finest rope handles ever seen, this vessel in cake-decoration style (rounded, applied strips) has a lively two-layer effect and controlled plastic surface. Miyanomae, Nagano. Height 59.5cm.

Middle Jomon

J72

J72   Kasori E (Ubayama) type. Pinpoint marks seem to serve in lieu of cord-marking on this two-handled vessel. The symmetry of the handles is part of a reaction that leads back toward balanced and modestly decorated pots in the latter half of Middle Jomon. The continuous patterns seem to have been selected for their curvilinear interest rather than displaying the panel concept of the Katsuzaka family pottery. Togariishi, Nagano-ken. Height 21.8cm.

Late Jomon

J73

J74

J75

J76

J73 Shomyoji type. Perfect symmetry in large vessels was very difficult to achieve for Jomon potters, as this unstable example from the highly productive Shomyoji shell-mound shows. There is some ambiguity in the cord-marking of the loosely defined zones. Shomyoji, Kanagawa-ken. Height 52.0cm.

J74 Horinouchi 1 or Shomyoji type. This vessel was unearthed at the 1959 excavation of the Soya shell-mound, standing upright about two metres outside a pit-dwelling. It contained bones assumed to be those of a new-born child. The freely incised decoration was laid out in zones but never cord-marked. Soya, Chiba-ken. Height 31.0cm.

J75 Horinouchi 2 type. Technical improvements in Late Jomon brought progressively thinner walls, accompanied by smaller vessels and narrowed bands of decoration. These are filled with cord-marking or a reasonable facsimile. A groove inside the rim was fashionable. Ubayama, Chiba-ken. Height 29.0cm.

J76 Horinouchi type. The Horinouchi type includes rather refined, overall cord-marking over which grouped parallel lines and space-filling spirals are incised. The rim is modest and joined by a vertical, notched ridge. Kanazawacho, Kanagawa-ken. Height 47.5cm.

Late Jomon

J77

J78

J79

J80

J77 Horinouchi type. This little cup with perforated base, light-brown colour and somewhat smoothed surface is typical of the modest decoration of Late Jomon and the interest in experimenting with shapes of vessels impractical for daily use. Grooving decoration is focused on the sides and on the slight rim-lip flares at either end. Hinoto, Iwate-ken. Height 13.4cm.

J78 Horinouchi type. Although the decoration is obviously closely related to the sharp ridges of the Daigi 8 type, the spout is poorly balanced for later Middle Jomon. The potter planned ways by which the lid could be secured in place. Batocho, Tochigi-ken. Height 12.0cm.

J79 Horinouchi type. This, like so many of the other pouring vessels, is a well-formed tea-kettle shape, the decoration done with much restraint. The handles and spout (here missing) were magnified as though to symbolize the vessel's distinctive use. Katabira Jinjakami, Kanagawa-ken. Height 19.5cm.

J80 Horinouchi type. Another of Late Jomon's curious creations, a human face on an 'incense burner' (the opposite side is open), this piece is an interesting departure from the type inherited from the mountainous region during Middle Jomon. With the addition of the stand, the incense burner or lamp takes on the fundamental form of all later examples. Kaizuka-cho, Chiba-ken. Height 16.0cm.

Late Jomon

J81

J82

J83

J84

J81 Tokoshinai 1 type. Late Jomon pottery has a less intimate, personal character, though at the same time it shows greater competence in handling of materials. Pots are usually fairly modest in size and rather thin-walled. Small bowls are now found in the same sites as pouring vessels. Tokoshinai, Aomori-ken. Height 12.0cm.

J82 Tokoshinai 5 type. Showing the rather narrow base characteristic of Late Jomon in the north, this regularly decorated vessel has the central constriction co-ordinated with the decoration above the midpart, thus keeping to a minimum the area of decoration that would come into contact with the cooking fire. Karumai, Iwate-ken. Height 34.0cm.

J83 Tokoshinai 1 type. Decoration on the Tokoshinai type is not necessarily ideally controlled, but it moves rapidly across the surface and never prevents the shape from being shown off to best advantage. Tokoshinai, Aomori-ken. Height 15.5cm.

J84 Kasori B type. Black. Inverted, broad smoothed lip. Side slightly curved inwards from the shoulder. Body cord-marked, grooved. Narita, Chiba-ken. Height 7.5cm, mouth diameter 13.0cm (K215 Kenrick Collection, Tokyo).

116

Late Jomon

J85

J86

J87

J88

J85 Kasori B 1 type. An all-purpose pot for cooking, storage of foods or water, this simple container has a slightly triangular shape to the rim and bears sketchily applied cord-marking in various oblique directions and more or less vertical, fine-line incising. It retains the rim ridge of Horinouchi type pottery. Soya, Chiba-ken. Height 42.5cm.

J86 Kasori B1 type. Better techniques now employed by the potters seem not to have necessarily fostered successful results in the experiments in new shapes for special functions. The results when using this as a pouring vessel should have been very interesting. Kamiyushizawa, Kanagawa-ken. Height 15.8cm.

J87 Kasori B type. The Fukuda shell-mound people experimented cautiously, making most of their vessels in rather simple, practical, tried and proven shapes. The size of the hole for the spout suggests that the spout would have been of moderate size. Four points are tied in with the outlines for the cord-marked zones, the cord-marking running in several directions. Fukuda, Ibaragi-ken. Height 12.5cm.

J88 Kasori B type. Although the Ubayama shell-mound is best known for its large yield of Middle Jomon vessels, many remarkable Late Jomon pieces have also come from this site. This pouring vessel of sharply angular outline, complemented by linear decoration, has a striking pair of high-set handles. The spout is a restoration. Ubayama, Chiba-ken. Height 16.0cm.

Late Jomon

J89

J90

J91

J92

J89 Kasori B type. A strangely shaped pourer, the spout would have had to be short for the vessel to maintain its balance. Some attempt had been made to clean off the broken area and attach a spout with the aid of pitch. The grooved registers are rough; alternate registers are smooth. Shiizuka; Ibaragi-ken.

J90 Kasori B type. The earliest 'incense burners' with side holes and pedestals appear at this time, although the lineage of the class of vessels can possibly be traced back to Middle Jomon 'lamps' in the Chubu region. The idea seems to move north from the shell-mound sites of the Kanto Plain. Fukuda, Ibaragi-ken. Height 16.8cm.

J91 Kasori B2 type. Handsomely waved, the narrow bands of minute cord-marking following the curve of the rim and linked together by figure-eight patterns, this fine vessel is one of many astonishing pieces from the Yoyama shell-mound in Chiba Prefecture. Yoyama, Chiba-ken. Height 14.6cm.

J92 Kasori B2 type bowls appear in a variety of shapes. This one with roller-coaster rim has strong oblique incisions as the chief wall decoration, a feature that is especially popular at the Omori shell-mound. Tachigi, Ibaragi-ken. Height 13.1cm.

Late Jomon

J93

J94

J95

J96

J93 Kasori B type. An attempt to be different ended with surprisingly good results – only one foot does not reach the ground. A well made and sturdy bowl, the smoothing was done with a hard-surfaced object, and tiny patches of overflow cord-marking went untouched. Shiizuka, Ibaragi-ken. Height 10.2cm.

J94 Kasori B2 type. A series of horizontal ridges furnishes a natural and pleasing set of proportions for this stemmed bowl, encircling the rim shoulder, neck and base of the stand. Regardless of variation in shape, the capacity of the bowls of this stage is remarkably equal. Yoyama, Chiba-ken. Height 23.5cm.

J95 Kasori B2 type. Vessels with this long, oblique hatching usually take the form of high bowls, often on a tubular base, or narrow vases with an exaggerated flare, as is seen here. Rims are more often waved or peaked. Tobe, Chiba-ken. Height 27.5cm.

J96 Kasori B2 type. The Shiizuka shell-mound, from which this vessel comes, is recorded as having been first dug around 1893. Many vessels and figurines have since been unearthed there. The incompletely defined zones of cord-marking tend to be late in the development of the zoned cord-marking style. Shiizuka, Ibaragi-ken. Height 22.2cm.

119

Late Jomon

J97

J98

J99

J100

J97   Kasori B3 type. Vessels distinguished by their simple shapes and coarse decoration were made for domestic use. Little time was wasted on their decoration other than for enough surface roughening to facilitate handling. Such purely functional vessels become part of the daily scene in the Late Jomon period. Kotehashi, Chiba-ken. Height 30.8cm.

J98   Tokoshinai 5 type. This vase may well be unique in being the only example with full figures on either side. Similar but not identical, they are finely cord-marked in more than one direction, as are the narrow horizontal bands and the loops that serve as their feet. Tokoshinai, Aomori-ken. Height 22.5cm.

J99   Oyu type. This bottle, a peculiar shape at this stage, with tree-like patterns rising off the midriff cord-marking, is just one more of the puzzling vessels from the Oyu stone-circle site, where the evidence of habitation is minimal, but all signs point to extensive ritual activity. Oyu, Akita-ken. Height 14.6cm.

J100   Oyu type. Vessels from Oyu display a variety of unconventional shapes, for which ingenious adaptations of ornamentation were required. Parallel incised lines or zoned cord-marking were used extensively; much less common in the Tohoku region is this sagging globular shape and squared rim. Nanukaichi, Akita-ken. Height 27.3cm.

Late Jomon

J101

J102

J104

J103

J101 Angyo or Kasori B type, early. This pot has lost its upper part, somewhat trumpet-shaped, above its present rim. Reddish with black areas, inside black. Flat, receding lip, slightly bulging shoulder tapering to a flat base. Short vertical grooves below the rim in an encircling indentation above diagonal, curving grooves on the body. Abiko, Chiba-ken. Height 15.2cm, mouth diameter 13cm (K085 Kenrick Collection, Tokyo).

J102 Angyo 1 type. Bowls on perforated stands are one of the more interesting innovations of the last stages of Late Jomon. This one probably comes from a large shell-mound in the eastern Kanto Plain. It has low ridges of square section, horizontally slashed, and joined near the holes by clay knobs. Height 14.8cm.

J103 Angyo 2 type. The Yoyama shell-mound, where this vessel was found, was formed during Late and Latest Jomon. Large, knobby rim projections are a borderline characteristic between the two periods and may be the only plastic feature on an entire vessel. Yoyama, Chiba-ken. Height 10.9cm.

J104 Angyo 2 type. The square-sectioned ridges with fine indentations are the Angyo 2 trademark. Some cord-marking was used, but it is largely obscured by freely incised, oblique lines. Nado, Chiba-ken. Height 36.1cm.

121

Late Jomon

J105

J106

J107

J108

J105 Angyo 1 type. So-called incense burners come from sites – mostly shell-mounds – in Chiba, Saitama and Tokyo prefectures. Their actual use is uncertain, but all are rather small. This particular one looks as though it could be inverted and be equally as useful. Yoyama, Chiba-ken. Height 16.0cm.

J106 Angyo 2 type. This pouring vessel has a rugged appearance with its sharply broken rim lines, the arrangement of ridges and knobs resembling a net and knots. The phallic spout is borrowed from the north, but now done in a less specific way. Fukuda, Ibaragi-ken. Height 12.2cm.

J107 Shinchi (t) type. Potted and combed by a very sure hand, this vessel – twice the size of the averge cooking-pot – was probably used by a relatively large family. Blackened areas above the foot lead one to suspect that the pot was placed upright in the ground. Sanganji, Fukushima. Height 48.5cm.

J108 Shinchi (t) type. This is one of the more bizarre creations of Late Jomon, reminiscent of the Han dynasty 'hill censers'. The limited number of motifs and accepted effects of paired knobs at junctures of cord-marked zones gives the decoration a coherence that did not exist before this time. Ohira, Fukushima. Height 10.8cm.

Final Jomon

J109

J110

J111

J112

J109   Obora B type. Vessels from Obora shell-mound tend to be larger on the average than most northern pots at this stage. A cooking-pot here illustrates the continuous production of utilitarian containers, a category of vessels overshadowed by the more interesting, elaborately decorated vessels. Obora, Iwate-ken. Height 38.1cm.

J110   Obora B2 type. Dated near the beginning of the long development of pouring vessels in the north, this piece shows the more globular southern shape, with proportions and placement of the spout that are more northern. The surface, however, is poorly finished for northern work. Ono, Akita-ken. Height 13.4cm.

J111   Obora B-C type. Vessels of this shape may have exceedingly thin walls and be brittle and easily broken. Here cord-marking appears around the rim and on alternate, horizontal bands of decoration composed of rhythmically interlocked S-like motifs. Ishinadate, Akita-ken. Height 27.0cm.

J112   Obora B-C type. This vessel is a typical shape of north Japan at the opening of Final Jomon. The principle of decorating such a shape seems to have changed from full surface coverage to two registers of repeated motifs, each of different size, occasioning a complex rhythmical system. Nakai, Aomori-ken.

Final Jomon

J113

J114

J115

J116

J113 Obora B-C type. This is another of the small Amataki vessels, named after this site where the excision technique is especially prominent. Long, interlocked S-shapes form the prime motif – to which all other details are strictly supplementary space-fillers. Amataki, Iwate-ken. Height 6.3cm.

J114 Obora B-C type. This is an excellent example of the chief motif repeated in two registers on a fixed scale – reduced on the lower register only enough to conform to the narrowing shape – hence a simple rhythm throughout. Spaces around the shorter 'worms' on the lower register are filled by one bump less than in the upper register. Amataki, Iwate-ken. Height 10.0cm.

J115 Obora B-C type. Amataki pottery shows remarkable workmanship, especially in the minute detail. Fine cord-marking is here combined with the carving technique to produce a very attractive bowl. Amataki, Iwate-ken. Height 6.1cm.

J116 Obora B-C type. Multi-directional cord-marking on the body's serpentine designs is another example of the fact that the Amataki site has yielded all variations of the current modes of decoration. More than sixty tiny waves decorate the rim. Amataki, Iwate-ken. Height 7.9cm.

124

Final Jomon

J117   J118

J119   J120

J117   Obora B type. Smallish jar with inside clay reddish/brown with blackened patches, outer surface almost all blackened. Wide mouth, serrated rim, bulging side receding to a small, slightly raised foot. Diagonal cord-marking over whole surface. Ainataki, Iwate-ken. Height 12.8cm, mouth diameter 16.0cm (K233 Kenrick Collection, Tokyo).

J118   Obora B-C type. Small pedestalled jar. Light brown, smooth, undecorated, wide mouth, inward curving side on small flat foot. Iwate-ken. Height 5.5cm (K235 Kenrick Collection, Tokyo).

J119   Obora C2 type. Buff-coloured bowl. Medium size. Flat, smoothed rim. Side curved to a small base. Vertical cord-marking over entire surface. Ainataki, Iwate-ken. Height 10.4cm, mouth diameter 14.3cm (K234 Kenrick Collection, Tokyo).

J120   Angyo 2 (?) type. This interesting creation is ostensibly a bowl with handle, but it cannot be used satisfactorily for drinking, nor does it seem very practical for transferring liquids from one container to another. The wormy decoration is almost unique; the rim projections may be the ultimate clue to its type. Shimpukuji, Saitama-ken. Height 6.0cm.

Final Jomon

J121

J122

J123

J124

J121 Obora B type. The many northern 'incense burners' have by this time become standardized as a cup on a pedestal, having a cone-shaped top with a pair of large, oval holes. Most are crowned with rather elaborately sculptured peaks. Nakayama, Akita-ken. Height 18cm.

J122 Obora B-C type. Minor variations on this bottle shape in the three northern prefectures of the Tohoku region are well known. They remind one of the sake bottle of today, and could well have been used at that time to contain a special drink. Nakayama, Akita-ken. Height 17.3cm.

J123 and **J124** Obora B-C type. An odd, lamplike object of fairly large size that can be held easily by the projecting part. This piece has a dolphin like motif, rows of squarish projections, the fanciful, broken outline of the rims of northern pottery, and a highly polished surface. It was an exercise in technical virtuosity. Kamiyashiki, Aomori-ken. Height 9.5cm.

Final Jomon

J125 & J126

J127

J128

J129

J125 Obora B-C type. Much of this vessel has little more than ornamental use, since it cannot be filled much above the rounded base because of the position and length of the spout. The capacity is therefore reduced to the size of a cup, giving rise to the idea that these are actually drinking vessels. Yokamachi, Aomori-ken. Height 11.7cm.

J126 Obora B-C type. Spouted vessels like this, which look as though the upper part had been forced down into the lower part, have a truncated appearance as though designed to take a lid. Entirely unbroken rims are a rare phenomenon by this time in the Tohoku region. Yawata, Aomori-ken. Height 10.0cm.

J127 Obora C1 type. Most of these vessels have low-slung proportions, short spouts following closely the rising curve of the body, and rather strongly projected, excised decoration encircling the 'waist' at the juncture of the high, rounded base and the concave body. Tokoshinai, Aomori-ken. Height 9.5cm.

J128 Obora B-C2 type. The decoration-covered base of so many bowls in the north leads one to believe that there must have been considerable sedentary appreciation of their beauty – not too unlike the formality of the tea ceremony of later historic times. Chojayashiki, Iwate-ken. Height 5.3cm.

J129 Obora C2 type. Bases of bowls in Final Jomon in the north are often quite picturesque, frequently bearing a continuation of the main decoration. Four tiny feet terminate the leaf-like, incised patterns. Height 7.7cm, mouth diameter 18.8cm.

Final Jomon

J130

J131

J132

J133

J130   Obora C1 type. One commonly held belief is that Final Jomon in the north is a period of declining creativity, socially cramped by its rituals, evidence of which is the great number of peculiar vessels and the obvious tendency to devote an overwhelming amount of attention to the exhibition of pottery skills. This cup on a high base illustrates a full mastery of pottery techniques. Hiranuma, Aomori-ken. Height 25.0cm.

J131   Obora C1 type. The cord-marked motif is repeated six times around the body; above, notched, irregular ridges are joined at periodic intervals. On the lower body of the opposite side of this piece is a small hole made after firing around which can be seen some asphalt, apparently once used as a glue. Higashizage, Akita-ken. Height 17.0cm.

J132   Obora C1 type. Rather peculiar in shape – at a time when the peculiar was becoming commonplace – this piece might perhaps be described as a wide-mouthed vase. The neck is cut back and smoothed, and cord-marking covers the underside. Ono, Akita-ken. Height 11.4cm.

J133   Obora C2 type. The 'flowing water' design rarely covers the entire body, making this vessel quite unusual. The decoration here is less precise than on most examples of the type. Botan-batake, Iwate-ken. Height 14.0cm.

Final Jomon

J134

J135

J136

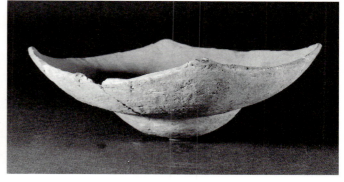

J137

J134   Obora A1 type. This decoration represents the most advanced and stylized form of the 'flowing water' design, a design normally limited to the upper shoulder of the vessel and measured off to fit the circumference exactly. Hachigasaki, Aomori-ken. Height 20.0cm.

J135   Kashiwara type. Kashiwara traits include imprecise shapes, rough surfaces requiring deep punctation to enable the decoration to be adequately seen, and a size that is easily held in the hand. The workmanship is slipshod. The nature of the site leads one to feel that the vessels may have had a votive use. Kashiwara Shrine park, Nara. Height 11.7cm.

J136   Kashiwara type. The work in the Kansai area and south stands in sharp contrast to the northern craftsmanship at this time. There is little interest in finishing the surface and experimenting with shapes, the clays become increasingly coarse, and the vessels vary little from basic utilitarian shapes. Kashiwara Shrine park, Nara.

J137   Kashiwara type. Decoration on vessels from the Kashiwara site ranges from relatively modest to completely plain. This round-bottomed bowl with ornamental rim would certainly not be easy to use. Kashiwara Shrine park, Nara.

Dogu and Masks

J138

J139

J140

J141

J138   Head and torso of subhuman figurine, from Misaka-machi, Higashi-yatsushiro-gun, Yamanashi-ken. Middle Jomon. National Museum, Tokyo. Height 25.5cm.

J139   Figurine from Shiizuka shell-mound, Edozaki-machi, Inashiki-gun, Ibaragi-ken. Late Jomon. Osaka City Art Museum. Height 12.1cm.

J140   Figurine from Satohara, Agatsuma-machi, Agatsuma-gun, Gumma-ken. Late Jomon. Collection Mr Yoshio Yamazaki. Height 31cm.

J141   Bell-shaped hollow figurine from Koshigoe, Maruko-machi, Chiisagata-gun, Nagano-ken. Late to Final Jomon, National Museum, Tokyo. Height 36.6cm.

Dogu

J142 (a)

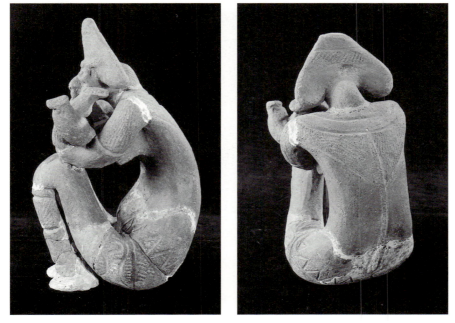

J142 (b)   J142 (c)

J142 (a, b, c) Crouching figurine from Hiagashi-yuno, Iizuka-machi, Shinobu-gun, Fukushima-ken. Late Jomon. Collection Mr Ishichi Ohara. Height 21.5cm.

131

Dogu

J143 J144

J145 J146

J143 Figurine with traces of red paint, from Hihara, Mishima village, Onuma county, Fukushima-ken. Final Jomon. National Museum, Tokyo. Height 27.4cm.

J144 Figurine from Shimpukuji shell-mound, Kashiwazaki-machi, Iwatsuki-shi, Saitama-ken. Final Jomon. Collection Mr Takeo Nakazawa. Height 20.4cm.

J145 Red-painted figurine from Konosu-shi, Kita-adachi-gun, Saitama-ken. Final Jomon. National Museum, Tokyo. Height 18.2cm.

J146 Hollow figurine from Ishinadate, Rokugo-machi, Senboku-gun, Akita-ken. Final Jomon. National Museum, Tokyo. Height 17.8cm.

132

Dogu

J147

J148

J150 & J151

J149

J147 Hollow figurine from Sarugamori, Tokoshinai, Susono, Hirosaki-shi, Aomori-ken. Final Jomon. Institute of Anthropology, Tokyo University. Height 12.7cm.

J148 Figurine with traces of red paint, from Japan Ironworks Co., Rinsei-cho, Muroran-shi, Hokkaido. Final Jomon. National Museum, Tokyo. Height 19.0cm.

J149 Figurine from Tateishi, Ajigasawa-machi, Nishi-tsugaru county, Aomori-ken. Final Jomon. Osaka City Art Museum. Height 19.3cm.

J150 Dogu head. Middle Jomon. Reddish. Prominent eyebrows. Ibaragi-ken. Height 4.2cm (K005 Kenrick Collection, Tokyo).

J151 Dogu head. Final Jomon. Reddish. Imaginative. Kamegaoka type. Aomori-ken. Height 4.9cm (K006 Kenrick Collection, Tokyo).

Dogu and Masks

J152

J153

J154

J152 Human-faced quadruped from Numazu shell-mound, Inai-mura, Ojika-gun, Miyagi-ken. Final Jomon. Institute of Archaeology, Tohoku University. Length 8.5cm.

J153 Clay mask from Kamegaoka, Kizukuri-machi, Nishi-tsugaru county, Aomori-ken. Final Jomon. National Museum, Tokyo. Height 10.8cm.

J154 Clay plaque from Fukuda shell-mound, Osuga-mura, Inashiki-gun, Ibaragi-ken. Late Jomon. Collection Mr Tsuneichi Inoue. Length 16.6cm.

Cord-marking and other texturing techniques

The following six pages give 94 examples of cord and other marking from Sahara (1981) without embarking on a book-length, English language description of their construction and characteristics. In Sahara's illustrations the direction of the twists is noted by L for left to right, and R for right to left.

The first four pages of Sahara's illustrations show cord-mark variations. The fifth page gives examples of cord-wrapped-stick marks and includes, No. 94, a squarish stemmed plant, shiso, used for impressing instead of cord. The sixth illustrates rouletting with a carved stick, Nos 96–104; shell-markings, nos 105–7, and various effects made with bamboo – in nos 108 and 109 rings have been cut from a small species of bamboo and fitted onto another stick; Nos 110–12 show the results of stabbing and dragging together; in no. 112 the addition of clay appliqué embellishes the design.

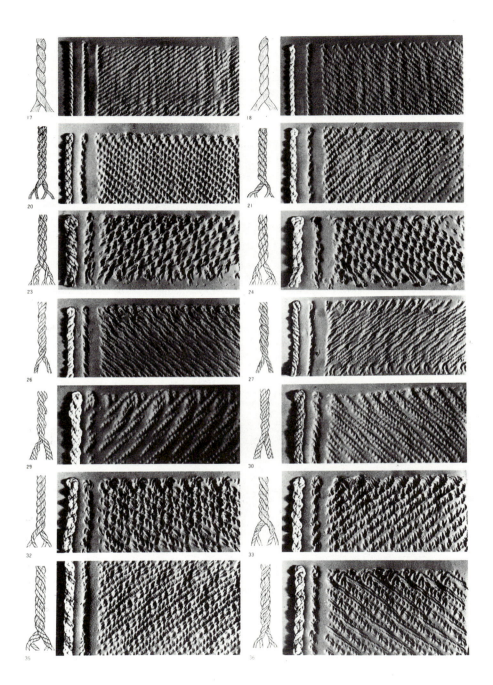

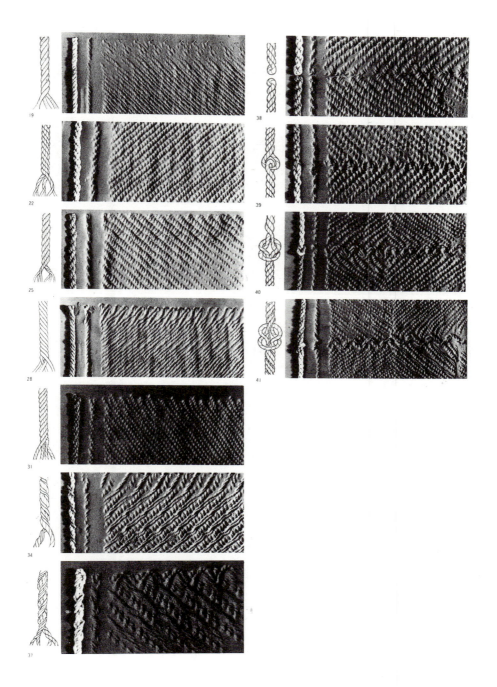

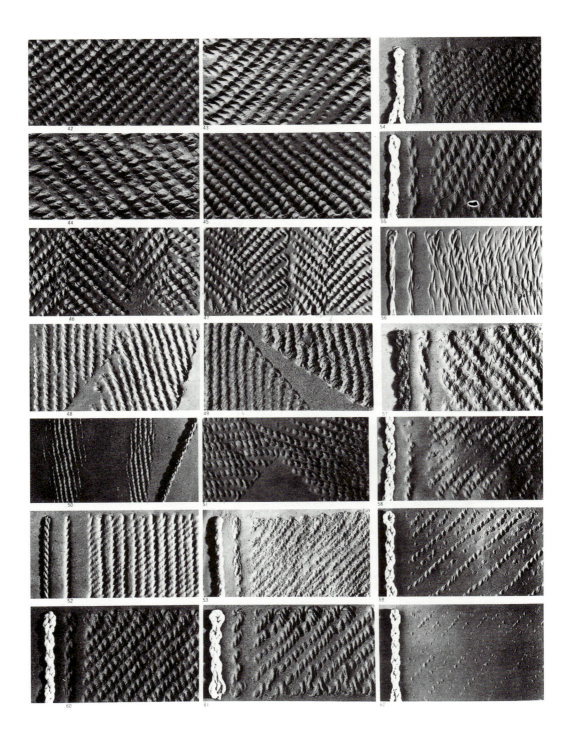

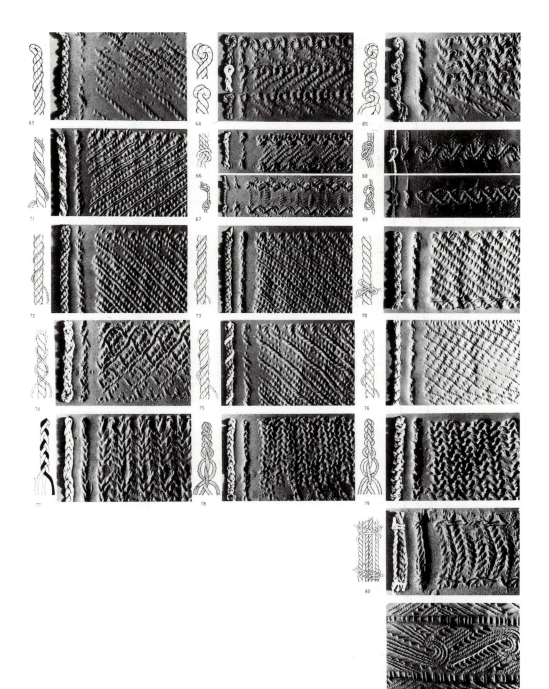

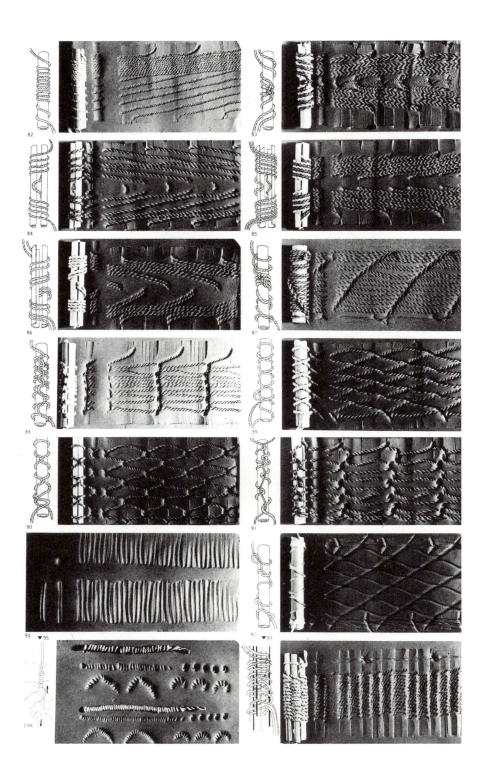

82

83

84

85

86

87

88

89

90

91

94 ▼95

198 ↓

92 ▼93

140

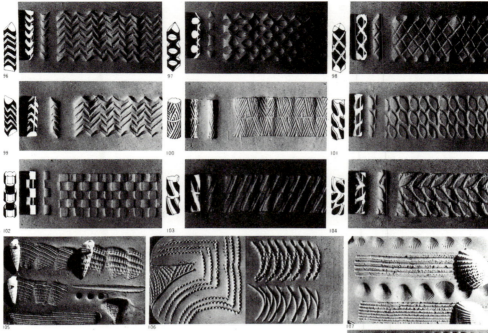

Index

Excluded are: Location, site, style and type names mentioned in the end notes, or in illustration captions, or those in the text but of secondary significance.